I0414299

Table of Contents

VII.   Exhibits

A.   Organizational Chart
B.   Summary of Requirements
C.   FY 2018 Program Increases/Offsets by Decision Unit
D.   Resources by DOJ Strategic Goal/Objective – Not Applicable
E.   Justification for Technical and Base Adjustments
F.   Crosswalk of 2016 Availability
G.   Crosswalk of 2017 Availability
H.   Summary of Reimbursable Resources
I.   Detail of Permanent Positions by Category
J.   Financial Analysis of Program Changes
K.   Summary of Requirements by Object Class
L.   Status of Congressionally Requested Studies, Reports, and Evaluations

I. Overview for the United States Marshals Service (USMS)

A. Introduction

The USMS requests $1,252,000,000 for the Salaries and Expenses (S&E) appropriation to fund 4,982 positions, 3,708 Deputy U.S. Marshals (DUSMs), 22 Attorneys, and 4,802 full time equivalent (FTE) excluding reimbursable FTE. This request is an increase of $23,758,000 from the FY 2017 Continuing Resolution. The Adjustments to Base (ATBs) include a Department-wide workforce rightsizing initiative mandated by the Attorney General, which translates into a USMS reduction of 572 positions, 426 DUSMs, and 74 FTEs.

The USMS also requests $14,971,000 for the Construction appropriation, equal to the FY 2017 Continuing Resolution.

Budget	Salaries & Expenses			Construction	Total
	Positions	FTE	Amount ($000)	Amount ($000)	Amount ($000)
FY 2016 Enacted	5,554	4,876	$1,230,581	$15,000	$1,245,581
FY 2017 Request	5,554	4,876	$1,228,242	$14,971	$1,243,213
FY 2018 Request	4,982	4,802	$1,252,000	$14,971	$1,266,971

The USMS request includes 100 positions and approximately $115,009,000 for information technology (IT) program. The USMS supports major IT areas such as mission modernization (the Capture initiative), tactical radio infrastructure, IT helpdesk support, wide and local area networking, voice communications support for voice and video teleconferencing, Unified Financial Management System (UFMS) program implementation, secured systems for protective operations and other IT-related services performing security and associated functions supporting law enforcement missions and administrative operations.

Electronic copies of the Department of Justice's Congressional Budget Justifications and Capital Asset Plan and Business Case exhibits can be viewed or downloaded from the Internet using the Internet address: http://www.justice.gov/02organizations/bpp.htm.

B. Organizational Background

History

The Judiciary Act of 1789 established the original 13 federal judicial districts and called for appointment of a Marshal for each district. The Senate confirmed President Washington's nomination of the first Marshals on September 26, 1789.

The Attorney General began supervising the Marshals in 1861. Marshals have been under the purview of the Department of Justice (DOJ) since the Department's creation in 1870. In 1956, the Deputy Attorney General established the Executive Office for United States Marshals as the first organization to supervise the Marshals nationwide. On May 12, 1969, DOJ Order 415-69 established the U.S. Marshals Service, with its Director appointed by the Attorney General. On November 18, 1988, the USMS was officially established as a bureau within the Department under the authority and direction of the Attorney General with its Director appointed by the President.

Mission

As America's first federal law enforcement agency, the USMS is considered the Nation's Police Force, and is responsible for protecting, defending, and enforcing the American justice system. The USMS protects the judicial process, the cornerstone of American democracy. The USMS uses the influence and reach gained through its accomplished history and broad authority to collaborate with other federal, state, local, and international law enforcement agencies, as well as with concerned citizens and members of the judiciary, to form a united front against crime.

The USMS strategic plan identifies mission challenges and strategies to mitigate these challenges. This road map guides resource investment, establishes the steps to improve operational performance, and positions the USMS to meet future challenges. Over the past few years, USMS has successfully executed its broad mission authority even as executive mandates and congressional legislation have resulted in dynamic growth across program areas, often without the corresponding support infrastructure. To successfully implement the strategic plan while continuing to excel in executing the mission, transformational change is required. Therefore, the plan addresses workforce and infrastructure in addition to the mission areas.

U.S. Marshals Perform a Wide Range of Duties

The USMS is the nation's oldest and most versatile federal law enforcement agency. Since 1789, federal marshals have served the nation in a variety of vital law enforcement roles. The USMS consists of 94 district offices and personnel stationed at more than 400 locations throughout the 50 states, Puerto Rico, Guam, the Northern Mariana Islands, the Virgin Islands, and the District of Columbia Superior Court. A U.S. Marshal, who is appointed by the President or the Attorney General, heads each district. The USMS headquarters is located in the Washington, D.C. area.

The USMS occupies a uniquely central position in the federal justice system, and is involved in virtually every federal law enforcement initiative. Approximately 5,000 Deputy Marshals and career employees execute the following nationwide, day-to-day assignments:

- ➢ apprehending fugitives;
- ➢ executing court orders and arrest warrants;
- ➢ protecting members of the judicial family (judges, attorneys, witnesses, and jurors);
- ➢ providing physical security in courthouses;
- ➢ transporting and producing prisoners for court proceedings;
- ➢ safeguarding endangered government witnesses and their families; and
- ➢ seizing assets gained by illegal means, and providing for the custody, management, and disposal of forfeited assets.

All USMS duties and responsibilities emanate from its core mission to ensure the safe, effective functioning of the federal judicial process.

Fugitive Apprehension

Deputy U.S. Marshals can be found:

- conducting domestic and international fugitive investigations;

- working closely on fugitive task forces and special cases with local, state, federal, and international law enforcement agencies;

- planning and implementing extraditions and deportations of fugitives;

- conducting financial and technical surveillance on specific fugitive investigations; and

- serving court papers, which is also known as service of process.

Judicial and Courthouse Security

Deputy U.S. Marshals can be found:
- in court with defendants in custody;
- protecting judges, prosecutors and witnesses;
- conducting threat analyses and investigations;
- conducting courtroom and courthouse security;
- planning courthouse facility renovations;
- managing courthouse security systems; and
- conducting courthouse and residential security surveys.

Prisoner Security and Transportation

Deputy U.S. Marshals can be found:

- fingerprinting all defendants in the federal court system;

- securing prisoners and defendants in custody in the cellblock;

- transporting prisoners and defendants in custody between the jail and courthouse, between federal judicial districts and states;

- receiving prisoners from other federal law enforcement agencies;

- providing prisoner housing and other services related to federal detainees; and

- conducting jail inspections.

Protection of Witnesses

Deputy U.S. Marshals can be found:

- protecting government witnesses;

- producing protected witnesses for court proceedings, and

- re-documenting and relocating protected witnesses.

Asset Forfeiture

Deputy U.S. Marshals can be found:

- seizing, managing and disposing of forfeited assets.

Deputy Marshals can be found:

- performing security, rescue, and recovery activities for natural disasters and civil disturbances;

- planning and implementing emergency operations including Continuity of Government activities;

- performing audits and inspections of U.S. Marshals operations;

- providing protection for the Strategic National Stockpile; and

- protecting America through constant readiness, incident management, operations, and training critical to mission success.

U.S. Marshals Service Responds to Shifting Priorities

The role of the U.S. Marshals has profoundly impacted the history of the United States since the time when America was expanding across the continent into the western territories. With changes in prosecutorial emphasis, the mission of the USMS has transitioned as well. In more recent history, law enforcement priorities have shifted with changing social mandates. Examples include:

- In the 1960s, DUSMs provided security and escorted Ruby Bridges and James Meredith to school following federal court orders requiring segregated Southern schools and colleges to integrate.

- In 1973, the Drug Enforcement Administration (DEA) was created, resulting in a greater focus on drug-related arrests. The USMS immediately faced rapidly increasing numbers of drug-related detainees, protected witnesses, and fugitives.

- The Presidential Threat Protection Act of 2000 (Public Law (P.L.) 106-544) directed the USMS to provide assistance to state and local law enforcement agencies in the location and apprehension of their most violent fugitives. As a result, the USMS increased the size and effectiveness of its regional and district-based fugitive apprehension task forces, thus providing a critical "force multiplier" effect that aids in the reduction of violent crime across the nation.

- Expansion of illegal immigration enforcement activities, including the implementation of Operation Streamline in 2005, increased federal prosecutions of immigration offenders and resulted in a significant increase in the USMS' prisoner and fugitive workload along the Southwest Border.

- The Adam Walsh Child Protection and Safety Act of 2006 (AWA) (P.L. 109-248) strengthened federal penalties by making the failure to register (FTR) as a sex offender a federal offense. This Act directs the USMS to "assist jurisdictions in locating and apprehending sex offenders who violate sex offender registry requirements." In response, the USMS established the Sex Offender Investigative Branch (SOIB) and opened the National Sex Offender Targeting Center (NSOTC) to carry out its mission to protect the public by bringing non-compliant sex offenders to justice and targeting offenders who pose the most immediate danger to the public in general and to child victims in particular.

- The Child Protection Act of 2012 (P.L. 112-206) provides additional administrative authorities to prosecutors and law enforcement agencies to further combat sex crimes involving children, including administrative subpoena authority, to the USMS Director for cases involving unregistered sex offenders.

- The Justice for Victims of Trafficking Act of 2015 (P.L. 114-22) clarified USMS authority to assist state, local, and other federal law enforcement agencies in locating and recovering missing children upon request. Previously, the USMS was only authorized to assist with missing child cases in which a warrant was already in place for the suspected abductor/companion. This new authority eliminated the need for a warrant, allowing the USMS to immediately support missing child cases.

- In 2016, the International Megan's Law to Prevent Child Exploitation and Other Sexual Crimes Through Advanced Notification of Traveling Sex Offenders (P.L. 114-119) was enacted. This law assigned a critical role in vetting and providing notification of sex offenders traveling abroad to the USMS National Sex Offender Targeting Center (NSOTC). Under the law, the Department of Homeland Security (DHS) will operate an Angel Watch Center (AWC) within Immigration and Customs Enforcement (ICE). The AWC will provide the NSOTC manifests of registered sex offenders who have scheduled travel within 72 hours. The NSOTC is then required to vet the manifests to identify "covered sex offenders" (i.e., the victim is less than 18 years of age) for the AWC.

In addition to these priorities, because more federal resources are dedicated to apprehension and prosecution of suspected terrorists, the USMS is constantly assessing and responding to demands for high-level security required for many violent criminal and terrorist-related court proceedings.

C. USMS Budget

The USMS' total request of $1,266,971,000 consists of $1,252,000,000 for the S&E appropriation and $14,971,000 for the Construction appropriation. The requested funding provides the necessary resources for the USMS to maintain and enhance its core functions and increase priority areas. The chart below exhibits the cost distribution of base adjustments.

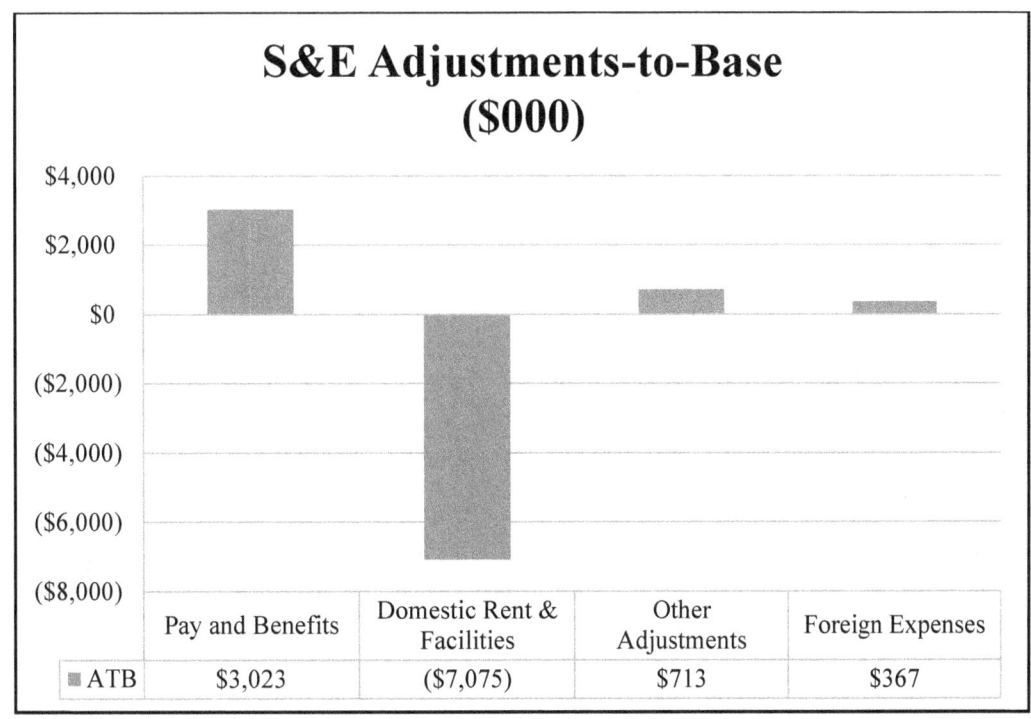

S&E Adjustments-to-Base ($000)

	Pay and Benefits	Domestic Rent & Facilities	Other Adjustments	Foreign Expenses
ATB	$3,023	($7,075)	$713	$367

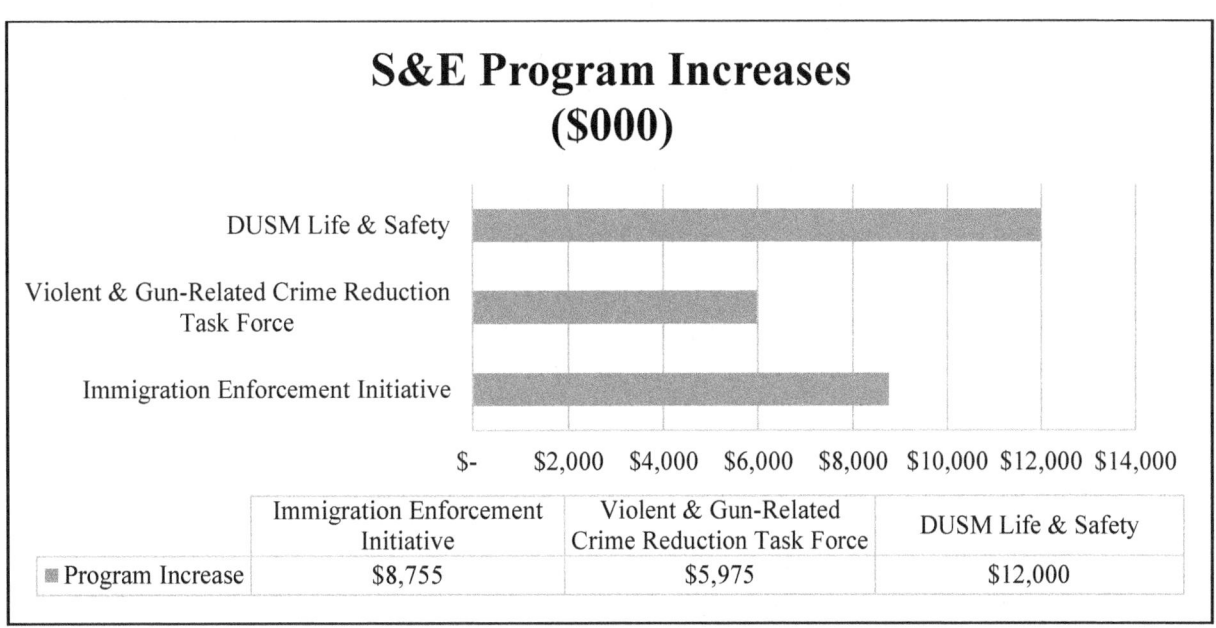

S&E Program Increases ($000)

	Immigration Enforcement Initiative	Violent & Gun-Related Crime Reduction Task Force	DUSM Life & Safety
Program Increase	$8,755	$5,975	$12,000

Total S&E ATBs for FY 2018 are a decrease of $2,972,000 from the FY 2017 Continuing Resolution funding level. The Construction request is equal to the FY 2017 Continuing Resolution funding level.

The USMS also receives reimbursable and other indirect resources from a variety of sources. Some of the larger sources include:

- The Administrative Office of the United States Courts (AOUSC) provides funding for administering the Judicial Facility Security Program.

- The Assets Forfeiture Fund (AFF) provides funding for managing and disposing seized assets.

- The Fees and Expenses of Witnesses (FEW) appropriation provides funding for securing and relocating protected witnesses.

- The Organized Crime Drug Enforcement Task Force (OCDETF) provides funding for apprehending major drug case fugitives.

The USMS S&E budget is divided into five decision units. These decision units contain the personnel and funds associated with the following missions:

- **Judicial and Courthouse Security (JCS)** – Ensures a safe and secure environment for federal judicial proceedings. Anticipates and deters threats to the judiciary; maintains the ability to deploy protective measures at any time; and, implements the necessary security measures for all federal court facilities.

- **Fugitive Apprehension (FA)** – Enhances the safety and security of our communities nationwide by locating and apprehending federal fugitives, egregious state or local fugitives, and non-compliant sex offenders. Creates and maintains cooperative working relationships with federal, state, local, and foreign law enforcement agencies; develops national expertise in sophisticated technical operations; conducts psychological assessments of sex offenders; and, collects and shares criminal intelligence. This decision unit includes management and disposal of DOJ's seized and forfeited assets.

- **Prisoner Security and Transportation (PST)** – Ensures safe and humane custody of all federal prisoners from time of arrest until the prisoner is acquitted, arrives at a designated Federal Bureau of Prisons facility to serve a sentence, or is otherwise ordered released from U.S. Marshal's custody. Provides housing, medical care, and transportation throughout the United States and its territories; produces prisoners for all court-ordered appearances; and, protects their civil rights throughout the judicial process.

- **Protection of Witnesses (PW)** – Provides for the security, health, and safety of government witnesses and their immediate dependents whose lives are in danger as a result of their testimony against drug traffickers, terrorists, organized crime members, and other major criminals.

- **Tactical Operations (TO)** – Ensures the USMS is able to respond immediately to any situation involving high-risk/sensitive law enforcement activities, national emergencies, civil disorders, or natural disasters. Maintains a specially trained and equipped tactical unit deployable at any time; provides explosive detection canines; operates a 24-hour Emergency Operations Center; and, ensures Incident Management Teams and Mobile Command Centers are always available.

The charts below represent the position and cost distribution by decision unit for FY 2018.

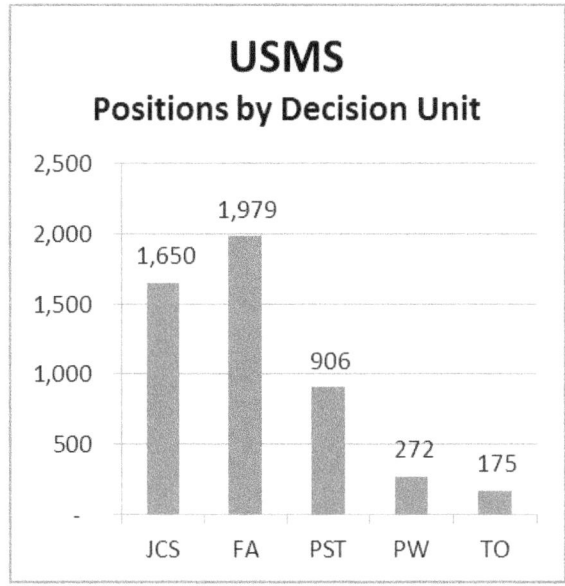

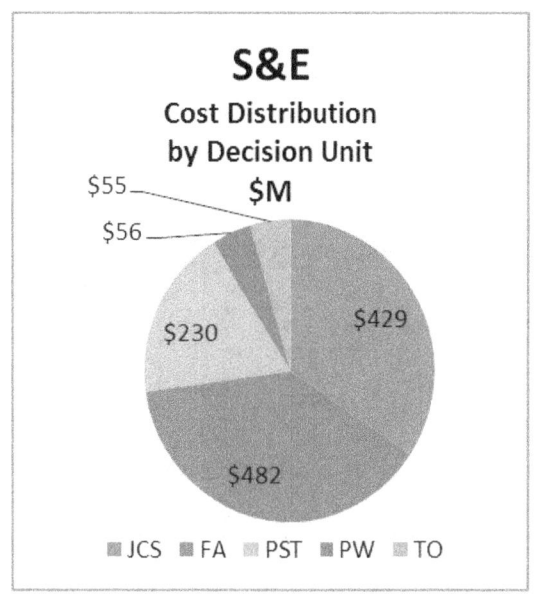

D. Sustainability

At the start of FY 2017, the USMS relocated to its new Headquarters in Arlington, Virginia. The relocation resulted in a reduction of 53,000 square feet of space. The USMS upcycled 1,289 pieces of furniture to the new building, and re-purposed 8,211 pieces of furniture by working with district offices, the General Services Administration (GSA), and other federal agencies. In addition, UNICOR recycled 1,335 pieces of old and obsolete electronics. The new Headquarters includes numerous energy efficient features such as daylight harvesting sensors, water conserving faucets, time zone and motion sensor Light Emitting Diode (LED) lighting, and energy-saving tinted window film. These improvements yielded a Leadership in Energy and Environmental Design (LEED) Certification from the GSA.

To increase sustainability, the USMS currently uses shared multifunctional devices (MFD) to print, copy, scan, and fax. The purchase of new, energy efficient MFD services allows the USMS to excess/recycle 962 smaller, less capable devices with a plan in place to excess/recycle an additional 178 units by the end of September 2017. Following completion of the second excess/recycle wave, only 40 individual devices will remain within headquarters. The new MFD units reduced build-out costs requiring less data drops and switch ports.

The USMS welcomes input from employees and members of its Green Team for innovative ideas promoting sustainability, energy and water conservation, and how to improve environmental awareness. The USMS has two Environmental Management System programs to help manage and track Greenhouse Gas emissions from its fleet of vehicles including aircraft operated by the Justice Prisoner and Alien Transportation System.

The USMS continues to encourage personnel to utilize teleworking, public transportation, ride sharing, or bicycling to commute to and from assigned work locations. In FY 2016, the USMS increased the number of employees participating in the federal transit subsidy program by 3.8 percent over FY 2015. In addition, telework participation increased by 138 percent from

FY 2015 to FY 2016. The USMS also received the 2016 Platinum Level award from Arlington County for implementing sustainable transportation programs including vanpools at the new Headquarters facility.

E. **Challenges**

The USMS continues to analyze cost savings measures for economies of scale; communicate transparently with the Department, Office of Management and Budget (OMB), and Congress; and pursue resources to accomplish the USMS' core mission, operate programs, improve detention management, ensure officer safety, and provide the highest possible security for the federal judicial process.

Mission Modernization

The USMS needs to modernize mission critical technology by upgrading operational infrastructure to increase operational and support effectiveness. The Justice Detainee Information System (JDIS) is the USMS' primary operational mission system. The current configuration and support for JDIS lack stability, scalability, centralization, and are no longer technologically sustainable. System capabilities do not meet current operational mission requirements effectively or efficiently. Moreover, JDIS does not easily interface with external local, state, and federal partners for complex data sharing.

Capture Initiative: In FY 2016, the USMS began to integrate required IT solutions with existing systems to maximize the government's return on investment. The development of Capture is expected to take four years at a cost of approximately $107,000,000. Capture incorporates a comprehensive integration and improvement of all current USMS operational business and mission capabilities (automated and manual), a consolidation of operational data, and an improvement of operational business processes at headquarters and in the field.

Since it is important to retire JDIS legacy system functionalities, the USMS has established a release plan for mission functions that consists of six deployments from FY 2018 to FY 2020. The transformation to implement Capture will be accomplished, in part, with a new web-based solution that enables user access from multiple platforms (i.e., desktops, tablets, and mobile phones) in a manner which is intuitive for each distinctive USMS line of business.

Today, if a deputy wants to retrieve all known data on a specific prisoner, they must access multiple applications on different systems and manually search filing cabinets to consolidate information about the detainee. Capture will implement an electronic master prisoner record which will provide biographic information, warrants, associates, detainees' current location, and other relevant details. Access to the master prisoner record will increase officer safety by making information about prisoner gang relationships, medical issues, or violent tendencies readily available. Deputies will access data using mission applications on the device that best supports their mission.

The USMS uses a line of business (LoB) model within Capture to ensure that it meets the needs of the organization. Three major LoBs support the activities of Salaries and Expenses decision units: Investigations, Security Management, and Prisoner Management.

- Investigations – This LoB links management, tracking, reporting, data interchange and administrative activities to support subject investigations, protective investigations, financial asset investigations, service of process, enforcement and tactical operations, and the implementation of the DOJ violent crime reduction strategy, as well as criminal intelligence collection and sharing that results from these activities. Other enforcement activities covered by this LoB include sex offender registry compliance checks; investigative activities such as electronic, air, and financial surveillance; and other agency resources that support investigations. In addition, the LoB includes Office of Emergency Management activities related to deployment of resources during times of crisis and natural disasters.

- Security Management – The Security Management LoB incorporates all activities related to securing spaces where a USMS footprint exists. This LoB is organized into four mission functions: Facility Management, Security Officer Management, Security Systems Management, and Protective Operations Management.

- Prisoner Management – This LoB spans the entire prisoner lifecycle from arrest through commitment and release, and encompasses medical support, prisoner transportation, and other logistics during imprisonment. Specifically, this LoB includes management of prisoner booking; custody and court case records; production of the detainee at trial appearances; designation of prisoners to facilities; facility vacancy management; and financial tracking of transportation costs with affiliated local, state, and federal agencies. Similar to other LoBs, Prisoner Management also contains reporting, data exchange, and administrative activities. Prisoner Management includes eight mission functions: Intakes, Custodies, Designation, Facilities and Inspections, Financial and Billing, Productions, Transportation and Medical Management.

Implementation of Capture is a mission-critical priority for the USMS. It will create efficiencies and benefit the USMS through:

- Significant improvement in operational business capabilities to enhance intelligence gathering, reporting, and decision-making that enhance and emphasize officer safety.

- Significant improvement in data management, retrieval, and reporting capabilities that make timely, integrated information available not only to the USMS but also to other federal, state, and local law enforcement agencies. As the USMS identifies and develops solutions beneficial to the USMS and the Department, it will strengthen its partnerships with DOJ components, other agencies, and state and local law enforcement. These efforts will improve the USMS' ability to discover information and generate knowledge, providing the USMS integrated, seamless, and reliable systems that are readily accessible to relevant data.

- Advanced enterprise data security which implements role-based access controls at the enterprise level, ensuring data can only be accessed by those with a need to know.

- Cost avoidance in man-hours spent manually searching, cleansing, consolidating, and analyzing data.

- Fielding integrated systems with configuration and support that are stable, scalable, centralized, and technologically sustainable.

- Reporting and analytics which will enable the integration of operational and administrative data management with analytical capability. This will include analytical tools, conversion to digital format, data sharing, electronic recording, geospatial map displays, search, security, data storage, and enterprise reporting.

Hiring Challenges

The USMS must establish a workforce structure that maximizes personnel availability for the full scope of duties and responsibilities throughout the agency. Hiring process regulations and the background investigation backlog are obstacles to staffing mission-critical positions.

The Office of Personnel Management (OPM)'s focus on increasing the number of applicants without streamlining applicant review, certification, and selection negatively affects the time required to fill vacancies without a measurable difference in applicant quality. To address the background investigation backlog, the USMS is exploring a variety of options: partnering with other DOJ components, working with OPM to alleviate bottlenecks, and seeking authority to conduct USMS background investigations.

Lack of excepted service hiring/appointment authority (EHA) and critical resources need to address the dynamic workload. The USMS faces a challenge in maintaining an agile hiring environment for law enforcement personnel, and requires additional resources to address changes from external workload drivers. Obtaining EHA for initial entry DUSMs will provide a more responsive hiring process, enable the USMS to react more quickly to changing hiring needs while retaining the merit principles of federal recruitment, and allow for targeted recruiting to strengthen diversity. In addition to these factors, the Department is pursuing EHA to achieve equity across all law enforcement components, establish a longer probationary evaluation period, and lower recruitment cost and time. The USMS also requires operational and administrative positions to respond to an uneven workload distribution that is driven by external factors such as crime initiatives, the number of arrests by federal law enforcement components, prosecutorial discretion, service of process requests, and judiciary resources.

Sound Cyclical Replacement of Mission-Critical Equipment

Resources for annual cyclical replacement of body armor, vehicles, radios, and surveillance equipment are imperative to ensure officer safety. Deputies and law enforcement partners also require regular, consistent training to maintain a culture of officer safety. USMS operational and technology infrastructure is stretched beyond its physical capacity. Protective gear, surveillance equipment, and vehicles are being used beyond their useful life cycles; and information technology infrastructure and communications have not kept up with technological advances.

Fugitive Apprehension

On the front lines every day, DUSMs reduce violent crime and make local communities safer. However, as society and technology evolve, even "routine" interactions with the criminal element become inherently dangerous. The USMS must continue to mitigate risk to its personnel and law enforcement partners by continuously reviewing and updating policies, procedures, equipment, and training as well as implementing a clear, consistent, standardized approach to fugitive apprehension in all scenarios, both within the United States and overseas.

Non-Compliant Sex Offenders

The Adam Walsh Child Protection and Safety Act (AWA) of 2006 designated the USMS as the lead law enforcement agency for apprehension of non-compliant sex offenders. Of the approximately 843,000 registered sex offenders nationwide, as many as 100,000 are estimated to be non-compliant with registration requirements. In response, the USMS has taken an aggressive approach toward protecting society from these violent offenders and child predators. While the USMS vigorously pursues AWA violators, these cases are becoming more complex.

Protecting the Judicial Process

The USMS must meet the challenges associated with an ever-expanding social media cyber threat and rapid technological enhancements. This includes having the very best intelligence, behavioral, and threat analysis; risk assessment methodologies; training of law enforcement and administrative personnel; maximizing workforce utilization; and, ensuring accountability and integrity of USMS programs, personnel, and financial activities through compliance review.

Intelligence Strategy

The change in terrorist tactics from large-scale attacks involving many actors to small-scale, individual attacks highlights the need for new intelligence resources to ensure the protection of the judicial process. By investing resources in positions, technology, and training, the USMS can leverage its unique position to gather information from fugitive investigations and interactions with detainees.

Investment in Security Systems

To address current and emerging threats, the USMS is engaged in a nationwide initiative to modernize physical access control of all court facilities. Modernization of courthouse Physical Access Control Systems (PACS) by the Administrative Office of the U.S. Courts (AOUSC) requires a large investment of resources by the USMS. The USMS needs to capitalize on this opportunity and address a long list of safety and security construction projects. Funding of both AOUSC PACS and USMS construction needs ensures efficient and effective projects that realize economies of scale and save the taxpayer money.

The USMS is employing a risk-based approach using the most up-to-date information available regarding current and future vulnerabilities and threats to prioritize the list of facilities. The goal is a more modern, reliable, and sustainable PACS which will strengthen the Judicial Facility Security Program (JFSP) and comply with all current federal policies, directives, guidelines, and standards governing the physical security of federal facilities. Additionally, employing an enterprise approach to administration and lifecycle management will result in more cost-effective and strategic responses to changing conditions and implementation of new technology.

Risk Management

The risk of continued employee misconduct, without proactive mitigation efforts, harms the public, the reputation of the USMS, and the Department of Justice. Use-of-force incidents and firearm discharges involving task force officers require timely investigation. USMS is working to expedite the review cycle and institute follow-up reviews to better mitigate agency-wide risks.

Detention Operations

Law enforcement and prosecutorial priorities and larger legislative reforms such as immigration reform, Southwest Border initiatives, and changes to sentencing guidelines directly impact USMS detention resource requirements. To meet these challenges, the USMS continues to reform business practices to optimize national detention operations. This transformation will include robust interagency and non-governmental collaboration efforts to develop innovative solutions that effectively forecast and manage prisoner processing, housing, transportation, and medical care.

II. Summary of Program Changes

Item Name	Description	Positions	FTE	Amount ($000)	Page
Deputy U.S. Marshal Life and Safety	For cyclical replacement of body armor, radios, vehicles, and surveillance equipment; and Special Operations Group (SOG) recertification and equipment. This funding would enable the USMS to replace mission critical equipment and maintain required tactical skills on a regular annual basis.	0	0	$12,000	68
Immigration Enforcement Initiative	To support the Administration's efforts to enhance border security and immigration enforcement. The USMS will increase the number of Deputy U.S. Marshals who apprehend and transport criminal aliens.	40	20	$8,755	77
Violent and Gun-Related Crime Reduction Task Force	Multi-agency focus on reducing violent and gun-related crime in hard-hit urban areas by using innovative means to locate individuals, organizations, and gangs within specific high crime jurisdictions. Resources will support short-term deployment of Federal law enforcement personnel to select urban areas to foster community awareness of criminal elements living, networking, and thriving in their communities.	0	0	$5,975	80

III. Appropriations Language and Analysis of Appropriations Language

United States Marshals Service

Salaries and Expenses

For necessary expenses of the United States Marshals Service, [$1,230,581,000]*$1,252,000,000* of which not to exceed $6,000 shall be available for official reception and representation expenses, and not to exceed $15,000,000 shall remain available until expended.

Construction

For construction in space controlled, occupied or utilized by the United States Marshals Service for prisoner holding and related support, [$15,000,000]*$14,971,000*, to remain available until expended.

Analysis of Appropriation Language

S&E: No substantive changes proposed.

Construction: For clarification purposes, the support costs related to the Construction Appropriation shall include contract-related costs that are necessary to efficiently and effectively manage the corresponding workload associated in executing these construction projects.

IV. Program Activity Justification

A. Judicial and Courthouse Security

Judicial and Courthouse Security	Direct Positions	Estimated FTE	Amount ($000)
2016 Enacted	2,222	1,880	$472,738
2017 Continuing Resolution	2,222	1,880	$463,366
Adjustments to Base and Technical Adjustments	(586)	(297)	($39,266)
2018 Current Services	1,636	1,583	$424,100
2018 Program Increases	14	7	$4,890
2018 Request	1,650	1,590	$428,990
Total Change 2017-2018	(572)	(290)	($34,376)

Construction	Direct Positions	Estimated FTE	Amount ($000)
2016 Enacted	0	0	$15,000
2017 Continuing Resolution	0	0	$14,971
Adjustments to Base and Technical Adjustments	0	0	$0
2018 Current Services	0	0	$14,971
2018 Program Increases	0	0	$0
2018 Request	0	0	$14,971
Total Change 2017-2018	0	0	$0

Judicial and Courthouse Security and Construction – TOTAL	Direct Positions	Estimated FTE	Amount ($000)
2016 Enacted	2,222	1,880	$487,738
2017 Continuing Resolution	2,222	1,880	$478,337
Adjustments to Base and Technical Adjustments	(586)	(297)	($39,266)
2018 Current Services	1,636	1,583	$439,071
2018 Program Increases	14	7	$4,890
2018 Request	1,650	1,590	$443,960
Total Change 2017-2018	(572)	(290)	($34,376)

Judicial and Courthouse Security – IT Breakout (of Decision Unit Total)	Direct Positions	Estimated FTE	Amount ($000)
2016 Enacted	41	41	$47,249
2017 Continuing Resolution	40	40	$43,095
Adjustments to Base and Technical Adjustments	0	0	$2,908
2018 Current Services	40	40	$46,003
2018 Program Increases	0	0	$0
2018 Request	40	40	$46,003
Total Change 2017-2018	0	0	$2,908

1. Program Description

The Judicial and Courthouse Security decision unit includes personal protection of federal jurists, court officers, and other threatened persons where criminal intimidation impedes the functioning of the judicial process or any other official proceeding or as directed by the Attorney General; facility security, including security equipment and systems to monitor and protect federal court facilities; and security of in-custody defendants during court proceedings.

The USMS establishes security by assessing the potential threat, developing security plans based on risks and threat levels, and assigning the level of appropriate security resources required to maintain a safe environment and protect the federal judicial process. High-security, high-profile events such as cases involving domestic and international terrorists, domestic and international organized criminal organizations, drug traffickers, gangs, and extremist groups require extensive operational planning and support from specially trained and equipped personnel.

To ensure that protected members of the judicial family remain unharmed and the judicial process is unimpeded, DUSMs are assigned to the 94 judicial districts (93 federal districts and the Superior Court of the District of Columbia). The USMS also assigns a Judicial Security Inspector (JSI) to each district to provide specialized knowledge, skills, and competencies for evaluating security at federal court facilities and off-site for judges, prosecutors, and other protectees. Additionally, the USMS has apportioned inspectors to each of the 12 judicial circuits to supervise protective operations when additional personal security is required due to threat-related activity.

Protective Intelligence

The USMS and FBI work together to assess and investigate all inappropriate communications received. The FBI has responsibility for investigating threats for the purpose of prosecution. The USMS conducts protective investigations that focus on determining a suspect's true intent, motive, and ability to harm the targeted individual, regardless of the possibility for prosecution. These investigations are the USMS' highest priority and involve the systematic discovery, collection, and assessment of available information.

The USMS' Office of Protective Intelligence (OPI) provides guidance and oversight to district offices for investigation of threats and inappropriate communications directed at USMS protected persons and facilities. The OPI serves as the central point of intelligence and information related to the safety and security of members of the judiciary and other USMS protectees. The protective intelligence information OPI collects, analyzes, and disseminates to districts ensures appropriate measures are put into place to protect the judicial process.

Judicial Facility Security Program

The USMS administers the JFSP, funded through the Court Security Appropriation within the federal judiciary. Central to JFSP's mission is the management of approximately 5,100 contracted Court Security Officers (CSOs) who provide physical security at more than 400 court facilities throughout the nation.

In addition to maintaining physical security of federal courthouses, the USMS develops and implements electronic security system installation plans to protect courthouses. These capabilities are critical to the safety of judicial officials, courtroom participants, the general public, and USMS personnel. Cameras, duress alarms, remote door openers, and other security devices improve overall security posture. When incidents occur, the USMS is equipped to record events, monitor personnel and prisoners, and send additional staff to identify and stabilize situations requiring a tactical response.

2. Performance and Resource Tables

	FY 2016		FY 2016		FY 2017		Current Services Adjustments and FY 2018 Program Changes		FY 2018 Request	
Total Costs and FTE (Reimbursable: FTE are included, but costs are bracketed and not included in totals)	FTE	Amount	FTE	Amount	FTE	Amount	FTE	Amount	FTE	Amount
	1,957	$472,738 [$11,166]	1,978	$482,869 [$4,739]	1,969	$463,366 [$13,506]	(278)	($34,376) [$0]	1,691	$428,990 [$13,506]

TYPE	PERFORMANCE		FY 2016		FY 2016		FY 2017		Current Services Adjustments and FY 2018 Program Changes		FY 2018 Request	
		FTE	Amount	FTE	Amount	FTE	Amount	FTE	Amount	FTE	Amount
Program Activity		1,957	$472,738 [$11,166]	1,978	$482,869 [$4,739]	1,969	$463,366 [$13,506]	(278)	($34,376) [$0]	1,691	$428,990 [$13,506]
Performance Measure: Workload	1. Inappropriate communications/threats to protected court members		1,930		2,357		3,112		0		3,112
Performance Measure: Output	2. Threats to protected court members investigated		593		384		525		0		525
Performance Measure: Output	3. Protective details required/provided to court members		25		14		25		0		25
Performance Measure: Outcome	4. Assaults against protected court members*		0		0		0		0		0

* Denotes inclusion in the DOJ Quarterly Status Report and DOJ Annual Performanace Plan

Data Definition, Validation, Verification, and Limitations:

Performance Measure – Workload

1. **Inappropriate communications/threats to protected court members:**

   a. **Data Definition:** The number of external events that require a protective assessment to determine if the event is a *security incident* – activity that requires documentation, but not further investigation (i.e. disruptive, suspicious, unauthorized persons or events); *preliminary assessment* – investigative activity that is done absent a triggering event. Requires some investigation and may require intelligence or behavioral analyses; or a *predicated protective investigation* – investigative activity where an adequate triggering event is present indicating a crime has or might take place. Requires a significant level of protective response to include comprehensive investigation and intelligence analysis; may involve behavioral analyses and/or protective measures such as a security detail, residential security survey, or security briefing. Success is defined as actuals below the estimate. Estimate represents maximum performance.

   b. **Data Validation and Verification:** Numbers are calculated based on reporting from the Justice Detainee Information System (JDIS) and are validated by the USMS Judicial Security Division.

   c. **Data Limitations:** This data is accessible to all districts and is updated as new information is collected. There may be a lag in the reporting of data.

Performance Measures – Outputs, Efficiencies, and Outcomes

2. **Threats to protected court members investigated:**

   a. **Data Definition:** The total number of predicated protective investigations opened which are investigative activities with an adequate triggering event, indicating a crime has occurred or might take place. Requires a significant level of protective response to include comprehensive investigation and intelligence analysis; may involve behavioral analyses and/or protective measures such as a security detail, residential security survey, or security briefing. Success is defined as actuals below the target. Target represents maximum performance.

   b. **Data Validation and Verification:** Numbers are calculated utilizing Justice Detainee Information System (JDIS) data and are validated by the USMS Judicial Security Division.

   c. **Data Limitations:** This data is accessible to all districts and updated as new information is collected. There may be a lag in the reporting of data.

25

3. **Protective details required/provided to court members:**

   a. **Data Definition:** A protective detail is a security assignment of 24-hour continuous detail or a portal-to-portal protective detail resulting from threat assessment. Success is defined as actuals below the target. Target represents maximum performance.

   b. **Data Validation and Verification:** Numbers are calculated utilizing Justice Detainee Information System (JDIS) data and are validated by the USMS Judicial Security Division.

   c. **Data Limitations:** This data is accessible to all districts and updated as new information is collected. There may be a lag in the reporting of data.

4. **Assaults against protected court members:**

   a. **Data Definition:** Includes criminal assault motivated by a protectee's status as federal jurists, court officers, and other threatened persons in the interest of justice, where criminal intimidation impedes on the functioning of the judicial process or any other official proceeding or as directed by the Attorney General and in-custody defendants during court proceedings. Success is defined as the actual meeting the target.

   b. **Data Validation and Verification:** Numbers are calculated utilizing Justice Detainee Information System (JDIS) data and are validated by the USMS Judicial Security Division.

   c. **Data Limitations:** This data is accessible to all districts and updated as new information is collected. There may be a lag in the reporting of data.

PERFORMANCE MEASURE TABLE

Decision Unit: Judicial and Courthouse Security

Performance Report and Performance Plan Targets	FY 2012	FY 2013	FY 2014	FY 2015	FY 2016		FY 2017	FY 2018
	Actual	Actual	Actual	Actual	Target	Actual	Target	Target
Performance Measure: Workload 1. Inappropriate communications/threats to protected court family members	N/A	1,155	768	926	1,930	2,357	3,112	3,112
Performance Measure: Output 2. Threats to protected court family members investigated	N/A	472	399	305	593	384	598	525
Performance Measure: Output 3. Protective details required/provided to court family members	N/A	28	13	17	25	14	25	25
Performance Measure: Outcome 4. Assaults against protected court family members*	N/A	0	0	0	0	0	0	0

N/A = Data unavailable
*Denotes inclusion in the DOJ Quarterly Status Reports and DOJ Annual Performance Plan

27

3. Performance, Resources, and Strategies

The USMS maintains the integrity of the federal judicial system by:

- ensuring that U.S. Courthouses, federal buildings, and leased facilities occupied by the federal judiciary and the USMS are secure and safe from intrusion by individuals and technological devices designed to disrupt the judicial process;

- guaranteeing that federal judges, attorneys, defendants, witnesses, jurors, and others can participate in uninterrupted court proceedings;

- assessing inappropriate communications and providing protective details to federal judges or other members of the judicial system;

- maintaining the custody, protection, and security of prisoners and the safety of material witnesses for appearance in court proceedings; and

- limiting opportunities for criminals to tamper with evidence or use intimidation, extortion, or bribery to corrupt judicial proceedings.

The USMS assesses the threat level at all high-risk proceedings, develops security plans, and assigns the commensurate security resources required to maintain a safe environment, including the possible temporary assignment of DUSMs from one district to another to enhance security. Where a proceeding is deemed high-risk, the USMS district staff and JSIs develop an operational plan well in advance of when a proceeding starts.

Measure: Assaults against court members
FY 2016 Target: 0
FY 2016 Actual: 0

Strategy: Develop standardized training programs on personal security awareness for the court family and protectees

The USMS delivers critical security awareness issues and best practices to USMS-protected persons through its successful video-based training program, "Project 365: Security Tips." The USMS expanded its offerings to the judicial family with the addition of a training video on active shooters and active threats. The "Active Shooter, Active Threat" video was produced by the Administrative Office of the United States Courts in cooperation with the USMS, and is designed to be a tool to assist in training the judicial family on how to respond to an active shooter or active threat event in a courthouse.

Strategy: Develop a continuing education strategy for all protectees on protective capabilities and procedures

The National Center for Judicial Security enhanced and strengthened the USMS's international presence by collaborating with the DOJ to conduct foreign trainings and assessments. The USMS conducted five training events and four court security assessments in Malaysia, El Salvador, Guatemala, Uganda, and Malta. To increase its reach, the USMS provided training that involved an overview on court security and personal security to North African judicial personnel attending a judicial conference in Malta.

Strategy: Formalize protective parameters for level of protection based on mitigation of efforts

The USMS established a training program on formal mitigation strategies. This includes OPI training, district protective investigations, JSI Basic and Sustainment training and Protective Intelligence Training Program (PITP) training. The positive feedback from training participants validates that USMS is better positioned to properly implement protection and creates greater standardization of protection parameters across the agency spectrum.

Strategy: Review and implement the results of reforms identified in the USMS Intelligence Assessment to determine applicable and approved intelligence and informational process recommendations which can be applied

The USMS improved intelligence-gathering capabilities through liaison positions with the National Joint Terrorism Task Force and the National Counter Terrorism Center. These liaison positions review information and intelligence and identify information that could impact USMS-protected persons or facilities. The relationships established by daily USMS presence at and interaction with the National Joint Terrorism Task Force and National Counter Terrorism Center have mitigated terrorism threats. The liaisons conduct research and collect information for dissemination to the USMS. They screen all source intelligence reporting, access summarized evaluated and previously-unevaluated information, discriminate threat information from all source intelligence into actionable intelligence, and disseminate warning and threat information to agency components.

Strategy: Providing security for the Supreme Court Judiciary

The USMS used the findings from a recently completed assessment on a risk-based protection program for the U.S. Supreme Court Judiciary to inform the development of a Memorandum of Understanding (MOU) with the Supreme Court of the United States Police Department. Upon signature, this MOU will clarify each agency's roles and responsibilities, identify new protocols to streamline communications, and standardize information sharing. Further, as a result of the assessment's findings, the USMS recommended significant updates to Executive and Judicial branch stakeholders to best provide comprehensive, routine protection for Supreme Court Justices.

Strategy: Leverage and/or partner with other agencies for physical security research and development needs

In FY 2016, the USMS established a liaison relationship with the Federal Protective Service. The liaison provides a direct link to Federal Protective Service stakeholders in the field, which allows for enhanced troubleshooting and de-confliction efforts. Furthermore, this relationship provides the USMS with FPS' Facility Security Assessment data, which is a contributing factor when prioritizing projects and enhancing understanding of security issues impacting the federal community as a whole.

Strategy: Assess the Court Security Officer (CSO) workforce and hiring practices to ensure mission needs are being met

Expediting the process for contract Court Security Officers (CSOs): The USMS designed and implemented a file-sharing system to allow for expedited submissions and approvals of contract CSO application packages. This streamlined process improves hiring efficiency and helps ensure consistent, full-coverage security services at courthouses.

Accelerating onboarding of CSOs: The USMS has decreased the backlog of CSOs awaiting Phase II Orientation by expanding each class size 40 percent, from 30 to 42 students. By the end of FY 2016, the backlog decreased 14 percent, or 72 students, from 517 to 445. The USMS also conducted regional training to meet immediate CSO needs in one district.

Strategy: Evaluate district management practices to establish a strategy to improve oversight of the Judicial Security mission

The USMS employs a dashboard tool to support district management. The USMS expanded the District Dashboard to include Quarterly Unannounced Testing results and statistics. This data aids in day-to-day judicial security oversight and provides transparency between geographically-dispersed judicial security management entities.

Strategy: Re-evaluate offsite security requirements, asset costs, and protocols to address current and future needs

The USMS improved off-site security program management for the Home Intrusion Detection Systems program by publishing new policy and developing business rules. The new policy and business rules allow the USMS to establish data collection points that will lead to improvements in decision making and the operational efficiency of the Home Intrusion Detection System program. The USMS continues to upgrade the technology of the Judicial Duress Alarm Response program, and is currently training Judicial Security Inspectors on the new technology.

B. Fugitive Apprehension

Fugitive Apprehension	Direct Positions	Estimated FTE	Amount ($000)
2016 Enacted	1,744	1,649	$416,216
2017 Continuing Resolution	1,744	1,649	$421,086
Adjustments to Base and Technical Adjustments	220	251	$48,286
2018 Current Services	1,964	1,900	$469,372
2018 Program Increases	15	7	$13,051
2018 Request	1,979	1,907	$482,423
Total Change 2017-2018	235	258	$61,337

Fugitive Apprehension – IT Breakout (of Decision Unit Total)	Direct Positions	Estimated FTE	Amount ($000)
2016 Enacted	33	33	$38,030
2017 Continuing Resolution	33	33	$35,554
Adjustments to Base and Technical Adjustments	0	0	$2,400
2018 Current Services	33	33	$37,954
2018 Program Increases	0	0	$0
2018 Request	33	33	$37,954
Total Change 2017-2018	0	0	$2,400

1. Program Description

The Fugitive Apprehension decision unit includes domestic and international fugitive investigations, fugitive extraditions and deportations, sex offender investigations, technical operations, and the management and disposal of seized and forfeited assets. The USMS is authorized to investigate such fugitive matters, both within and outside the United States, as directed by the Attorney General, although this authorization is not to be construed to interfere with or supersede the authority of other federal agencies or bureaus.

Domestic Fugitive Investigations

The USMS is the federal government's primary agency for apprehending fugitives and provides assistance and expertise to other federal, state, and local law enforcement agencies in support of fugitive investigations. The USMS works aggressively to reduce violent crime through the apprehension of fugitives using a nationwide network of task forces and other investigative resources such as criminal intelligence, electronic, air, and financial surveillance.

Currently, the USMS is the lead agency for 60 district-led fugitive task forces and seven

Regional Fugitive Task Forces (RFTFs). District task forces, composed of district USMS personnel and state and local law enforcement officers, investigate federal felony warrants where the USMS has execution authority and egregious state and local fugitives within the district. RFTFs partner with federal, state, and local law enforcement agencies and focus investigative resources to locate and apprehend the most egregious state and local fugitives within the task force's region, and to assist in high-profile investigations that identify criminal activities for future state and federal prosecutions. The nationwide network of USMS fugitive task forces focuses investigative efforts and resources to impact violent crime by targeting fugitives wanted for committing violent felony offenses.

The USMS prioritizes investigation and apprehension of some of the country's most dangerous fugitives by allocating resources and funding to its 15 Most Wanted Fugitive Program and Major Case Fugitive Program. These initiatives target high-profile offenders who tend to be career criminals with histories of violence and pose a significant threat to public safety.

In addition, the USMS is responsible for the majority of fugitive investigations conducted on behalf of the Organized Crime Drug Enforcement Task Force (OCDETF). In partnership with OCDETF, the USMS assists state and local partner agencies in apprehending numerous drug-related and organized crime felons who are eventually prosecuted at the state level.

International Fugitive Investigations

In addition to domestic investigations, the USMS investigates international fugitives.

The globalization of crime, coupled with the immediate mobility of fugitives, requires an intensive effort to identify, locate, apprehend, and remove transnational fugitives who flee the jurisdiction of one country only to seek refuge in another. The USMS developed several international fugitive programs to effectively combat this challenge. Resources committed to this mission include three foreign field offices, six regional desks at Headquarters, and the Canada and Mexico investigative liaison programs. Additionally, the USMS oversees liaison positions at INTERPOL–United States National Central Bureau (USNCB), the DOJ Office of International Affairs (OIA), and the El Paso Intelligence Center (EPIC). The USMS also provides direction, oversight, and training on international investigations and the extradition process to federal, state, local, and foreign law enforcement agencies and prosecutors' offices.

The USMS is the lead agency responsible for investigation and apprehension of international and foreign fugitives. Through MOUs with federal law enforcement agencies and from requesting state or local agencies, the USMS has apprehension responsibility for fugitives who leave the jurisdiction of the United States. Extraterritorial investigations are conducted in concert with other law enforcements agencies in countries lacking a USMS presence. Through agreements with USNCB, OIA, and foreign law enforcement authorities, the USMS also investigates foreign fugitives within the borders of the United States.

The USMS currently has an active caseload of approximately 55,800 fugitive cases. Of these, the International Investigations Branch (IIB) has open active investigations on more than 1,000 international fugitives who have fled the United States, and is also investigating over 200 fugitives wanted by foreign countries who are believed to be in the United States. The IIB also tracks fugitives who have valid U.S. warrants, but are currently unable to be returned to the United States due to limitations of bilateral treaties or cases not accepted for prosecution. These fugitives are tracked to ensure investigative due diligence for potential removal should circumstances change.

The management and execution of the U.S. Government's extradition program is a second critical mission. The USMS has statutory responsibility for conducting complex international extraditions from foreign countries to the United States on behalf of all federal, state, and local law enforcement agencies. The USMS manages extradition logistics through strong partnerships with OIA, U.S. law enforcement personnel abroad, and foreign authorities. The USMS reciprocates by assisting foreign authorities conducting extraditions from the United States.

Sex Offender Investigations

As the lead law enforcement agency responsible for investigating sex offender registration violations, the USMS has three distinct missions pursuant to the Adam Walsh Child Protection and Safety Act:

- assisting state, local, tribal, and territorial authorities in the location and apprehension of non-compliant sex offenders;
- investigating violations of 18 USC § 2250 and related offenses; and
- assisting in the identification and location of sex offenders relocated as a result of a major disaster.

The USMS carries out its duties in partnership with state, local, military, tribal, and territorial law enforcement authorities and works closely with the National Center for Missing and Exploited Children.

The USMS established the NSOTC to further enhance its capabilities and support state and local partners. The NSOTC and the USMS Sex Offender Investigation Coordinators in the field partner with the DOJ's Office of Sex Offender Sentencing, Monitoring, Apprehending, Registering, and Tracking (SMART) and agencies such as DOD, INTERPOL, the DOS-DSS, and Customs and Border Protection to identify, locate, and prosecute non-compliant sex offenders domestically and internationally. Additionally, the NSOTC now receives notification from the DOD's Military Correctional Branch when military convicted sex offenders are released, which allows enforcement officials to better identify non-compliant sex offenders for arrest and prosecution. Sex offender investigation activities also support the DOJ's National Strategy for Child Exploitation Prevention and Interdiction.

Technical Operations

The Technical Operations Group (TOG) provides the USMS, other federal agencies, and state or local law enforcement agencies with the most timely and technologically advanced electronic surveillance and investigative intelligence. TOG operates from eight Regional Technical Operations Centers (RTOCs) and 21 field offices throughout the United States and Mexico. Annually, the USMS assists hundreds of other federal, state, and local law enforcement agencies in support of thousands of the nation's most critical and time-sensitive investigations.

TOG comprises two branches that work synergistically – the Electronic Surveillance Branch (ESB) and the Air Surveillance Branch (ASB). The ESB provides state-of-the-art electronic surveillance assistance in fugitive investigations. It deploys sophisticated commercial and sensitive technical surveillance technologies for the interception of hard line and cellular telecommunications, Wi-Fi collection and emitter location, and Global Positioning System (GPS) and radio frequency tagging/tracking. The ESB also conducts computer and cellular exploitation and on-scene forensic extraction, photo/video surveillance, and Technical Surveillance and Countermeasure (TSCM) sweeps to detect surreptitious monitoring devices.

The ASB provides aerial support for missions throughout the USMS using specially-equipped fixed wing aircraft outfitted with advanced avionics, surveillance, and communications capabilities. The aircraft and pilots, co-located with the RTOCs, provide a variety of investigative, surveillance, and reconnaissance capabilities including still and motion aerial imagery and enhancement, aerial RF beacon tracking, mobile communication command and control, and electronic surveillance package deployment in support of fugitive investigative missions.

TOG is the USMS liaison to the U.S. Intelligence Community (IC) with respect to signal intelligence, measurement and signature intelligence, imagery intelligence, electronic intelligence, and communications intelligence. The USMS also shares its investigative tactics, techniques, and procedures with certain members of the IC and DOD. This collaborative effort has allowed all participants to enhance their capabilities and mission readiness.

Asset Forfeiture

The USMS serves as the primary custodian for the DOJ Asset Forfeiture Program (AFP), whose mission is to support the consistent and strategic use of asset forfeiture to disrupt and dismantle criminal enterprises, deprive wrongdoers of the profits and instrumentalities of criminal activity, deter crime, and restore property to victims of crime while protecting individual rights. The USMS provides fiduciary stewardship to ensure that assets seized for forfeiture are managed and disposed of efficiently and effectively. DOJ AFP participating agencies include DEA, FBI, ATF, FDA, DOS-DSS, DOD Criminal Investigation Service, U.S. Postal Inspection Service, and each of the U.S. Attorney's offices.

USMS Asset Forfeiture Financial Investigators (AFFI) proactively identify assets during investigations by working in conjunction with investigative agencies and U.S. Attorney's offices to conduct financial analyses that determine net equities of assets targeted for forfeiture, execute court orders, and assist in the physical seizure and security of the assets. AFFI positions are funded from the AFF, and work exclusively in the USMS AFP.

2. Performance and Resource Tables

PERFORMANCE AND RESOURCES TABLE

Decision Unit: Fugitive Apprehension

RESOURCES ($ in thousands)	Target FY 2016		Actual FY 2016		Target FY 2017		Changes Current Services Adjustments and FY 2018 Program Changes		Requested (Total) FY 2018 Request	
	FTE	Amount	FTE	Amount	FTE	Amount	FTE	Amount	FTE	Amount
Total Costs and FTE (Reimbursable: FTE are included, but costs are bracketed and not included in totals)	1,944	$416,216 [$12,974]	1,738	$436,547 [$8,715]	1,915	$421,086 [$13,280]	258	$0 [$0]	2,173	$482,423 [$13,280]

TYPE	PERFORMANCE	Target FY 2016		Actual FY 2016		Target FY 2017		Changes Current Services Adjustments and FY 2018 Program Changes		Requested (Total) FY 2018 Request	
		FTE	Amount	FTE	Amount	FTE	Amount	FTE	Amount	FTE	Amount
Program Activity		1,944	$416,216 [$12,974]	1,738	$436,547 [$8,715]	1,915	$421,086 [$13,280]	258	$0 [$0]	2,173	$482,423 [$13,280]
Performance Measure: Workload	1. Number of Federal fugitives		48,540		51,510		49,397		1,472		50,869
Performance Measure: Workload	2. Number of assets in inventory a. Cash b. Complex Assets c. All Other Assets		15,680 9,500 180 6,000		15,346 9,677 291 5,378		Retired		Retired		Retired
Performance Measure: Workload	3. Number of assets received* a. Cash b. Complex Assets c. All Other Assets		13,500 8,410 90 5,000		13,537 7,721 183 5,633		11,488 7,200 88 4,200		0 0 0 0		11,488 7,200 88 4,200
Performance Measure: Outcome	4. Number of Federal warrants cleared		30,144		34,537		30,794		917		31,711

N/A = Data Unavailable
* Denotes new measure

35

RESOURCES ($ in thousands)		Target	Actual	Target	Changes	Requested (Total)
TYPE	PERFORMANCE	FY 2016	FY 2016	FY 2017	Current Services Adjustments and FY 2018 Program Changes	FY 2018 Request
Performance Measure: Output	5. Non-Compliant Sex Offender Investigations	1,786	1,920	1,813	27	1,840
Performance Measure: Output	6. Number of assets disposed a. Cash b. Complex Assets c. All Other Assets	14,500 9,210 70 5,220	15,949 9,508 138 6,303	12,716 8,000 96 4,620	0 0 0 0	12,716 8,000 96 4,620
Performance Measure: Output	7. Percent of asset value returned to Fund*	55%	55%	Retired	Retired	Retired
Performance Measure: Output	8. Comparison of value returned to Fund** a. Jewelry, Arts, Antiques & Collectibles b. Real Property c. Vehicles	85% 75% 75%	89% 91% 85%	85% 75% 60%	0 0 0	85% 75% 60%
Performance Measure: Outcome	9. Percent of All Other Assets disposed within procedural time frames*	60%	55%	Retired	Retired	Retired
Performance Measure: Outcome	10. Assets disposed with Procedural Timeframes by Category** a. Real Property b. Conveyances (vehicles, vessels and aircraft)	80% 80%	54% 75%	75% 85%	0 0	75% 85%
Performance Measure: Outcome	11. Number of USMS federal and egregious non-federal fugitives apprehended/cleared	104,556	106,078	103,468	629	104,097
Performance Measure: Outcome	12. Number and percent Federal fugitives apprehended/cleared	29,124 60%	32,831 64%	29,638 60%	86 0	29,769 60%

* Denotes inclusion in the DOJ Quarterly Status Report
** Denotes new measure

Data Definition, Validation, Verification, and Limitations:

Performance Measures – Workload

1. **Federal fugitives:**

   a. **Data Definition:** Wanted fugitives include all those wanted at the beginning of the fiscal year, plus all fugitive cases received by the USMS throughout the fiscal year. Fugitives with multiple warrants are counted once.

   b. **Data Validation and Verification:** Warrant and fugitive data is verified by a random sampling of National Crime Information Center (NCIC) records generated by the FBI. The USMS coordinates with district offices to verify that warrants are validated against the signed paper records. The USMS then forwards the validated records back to NCIC.

   c. **Data Limitations:** Data is accessible to all districts and updated as new information is collected. There may be a reporting lag.

2. **Number of assets in inventory – Retired: Transition to *number of assets received*. Assets in inventory are a snapshot in time and therefore are limited in depicting workload variability.**

   a. **Data Definition:** The number of assets currently in USMS custody that are pending forfeiture decision/disposal instructions.

   b. **Data Validation and Verification:** Assets are recorded by seizing agencies and verified by District Offices. Data is entered by individuals in District Offices and Headquarters and is audited by internal and external controls.

   c. **Data Limitations:** Data is estimated based on the date extracted, as data entry in the Consolidated Asset Tracking System (CATS) is a continuous process.

3. **Number of assets received – includes a count of the number of assets received during the fiscal year.**

   a. **Data Definition (Cash):** The count of unique cash asset IDs received into USMS custody.

   Data Definition (Complex Assets): The number of assets IDs categorized as commercial business, financial instrument, or intangible asset received into USMS custody.

   Data Definition (All Other Assets): The total number of unique asset IDs, less cash and complex assets, received into USMS custody.

   b. **Data Validation and Verification:** Assets are recorded by seizing agencies and verified by District Offices. Data is entered by individuals in District Offices and Headquarters and is audited by internal and external controls.

   c. **Data Limitations:** Data is estimated based up the date extracted, as CATS data entry is continuous.

Performance Measures – Outputs, Efficiencies, and Outcomes

4. **Number of federal warrants cleared:**

   a. **Data Definition:** A warrant is considered cleared if the fugitive is arrested, has a detainer issued, or the warrant is dismissed.

   b. **Data Validation and Verification:** Warrant and fugitive data is verified by a random sampling of NCIC records generated by the FBI. The USMS coordinates with district offices to verify that warrants are validated against the signed paper records. The USMS then forwards the validated records back to NCIC.

   c. **Data Limitations:** Data is accessible to all districts and updated as new info is collected. There may be a reporting lag.

5. **Non-compliant sex offender investigations:**

   a. **Data Definition:** Opened investigations of violators of the Adam Walsh Child Protection and Safety Act that reach the level of the Attorney General's Guidelines for Conducting Domestic Investigations.

   b. **Data Validation and Verification:** Office of Compliance Review (OCR) annual Self-Assessment Guide (SAG) review of cases to DOJ and USMS policy and procedures. OCR also conducts annual on-site inspections of Districts and Divisions each year.

   c. **Data Limitations:** Data entry often lags behind operations causing a delay in timely and accurate information. This lag varies by office size, staffing and other intangibles.

6. **Number of assets disposed:**

   a. **Data Definition (Cash):** The count of unique cash asset IDs in USMS custody.

   Data Definition (Complex Asset): The number of assets IDs categorized as commercial business, financial instrument, or intangible asset received into USMS custody.

   Data Definition (All Other Assets): The total number of unique asset IDs, less cash and complex assets disposed.

   b. **Data Validation and Verification:** Assets are recorded by seizing agencies and verified by District Offices. Data is entered by individuals in District Offices and Headquarters and is audited by internal and external controls

   c. **Data Limitations:** Data is estimated based on the date extracted, as CATS data entry is continuous.

7. **Percent of asset value returned to the fund – Retired: Transition to *comparison of value returned to the fund*. Current measure accounts for victim payments and equitable sharing the same as maintenance and disposal costs.**

   a. **Data Definition:** The percent of asset value returned to the fund is calculated as value collected from the asset at disposal, less maintenance fees, victim payments, and equitable sharing; divided by value collected from the asset at disposal.

   b. **Data Validation and Verification:** Assets are recorded by seizing agencies and verified by District Offices. Data is entered by individuals in District Offices and Headquarters and is audited by internal and external controls.

   c. **Data Limitations:** Data is estimated based on the date extracted, as CATS data entry is continuous.

8. **Comparison of Value Returned to the Fund – New: Includes only assets disposed through sale. Calculations by asset category allow for the identification of specific performance trends.**

   a. **Data Definition (Jewelry, Arts, Antiques, and Collectibles):** The percent proceeds returned to the fund through the sale of Jewelry, Arts, Antiques, and Collectibles (JAAC). The percentage is calculated by sale value of the asset at disposal, less management and disposition fees; divided by the appraised value.

   b. **Data Definition (Real Property):** The percent proceeds returned to the fund through the sale of Real Property. The percentage is calculated as sale value of the asset at disposal, less management and disposition fees; divided by appraised value.

   c. **Data Definition (Vehicles):** The percent proceeds returned to the fund through the sale of Vehicles. The percentage is calculated as sale value of the asset at disposal, less management and disposition fees; divided by the appraised value.

   d. **Data Validation and Verification:** Assets are recorded by seizing agencies and verified by District Offices. Data is entered by individuals in District Offices and Headquarters and is audited by internal and external controls.

   e. **Data Limitations:** Data is estimated based on the date extracted, as CATS data entry is continuous.

9. **Percent of All Other Assets disposed within procedural time frames – Retired: Transition to *assets disposed within procedural timeframes by category* to better reflect performance for the majority of assets.**

   a. **Data Definition:** The number listed for "percent of all other assets disposed" signifies the total assets disposed within procedural timeframes.

   b. **Data Validation and Verification:** Data is estimated based on the date extracted, as CATS data entry is continuous.

   c. **Data Limitations:** Data is estimated based on the date extracted, as CATS data entry is continuous.

10. **Assets Disposed Within Procedural Timeframes by Category – New: Allows for performance trend identification for asset categories with differing procedural timeframes**

a. **Data Definition (Real Property):** The number of real property assets disposed within established procedural timeframes, divided by the total number of real property assets disposed.

Data Definition (Conveyances) [Vehicles, Vessels and Aircraft]: The number of conveyances disposed within established procedural timeframes, divided by the total number of conveyances disposed.

b. **Data Validation and Verification:** Data is estimated based on date extracted, as CATS data entry is continuous.

c. **Data Limitations:** Data is estimated based on the date extracted, as CATS data entry is continuous.

11. **Number of USMS federal and egregious non-federal fugitives apprehended/cleared:**

a. **Data Definition:** Includes physical arrest, directed arrest, surrender, dismissal, and arrest by another agency, when a federal fugitive is taken into custody on a detainment order, and warrants that are dismissed to the other cleared categories. It also includes egregious non-federal felony fugitives, including targeted state and local fugitives with an offense code of homicide, kidnapping, sexual assault, robbery, assault, threats, arson, extortion, burglary, vehicle theft, dangerous drugs, sex offenses, obscenity, family offenses, obstructing the police, escape, obstruction of justice, weapon offenses, and/or crime against persons.

b. **Data Validation and Verification:** See federal fugitives (warrants) above. Prior to assigning state and local warrants, the Supervisory Deputy U.S. Marshal (SDUSM) or designee is responsible for reviewing each case to verify it meets above criteria.

c. **Data Limitations:** Data is accessible to all districts and updated as new info is collected. There may be a reporting lag.

12. **Number and Percent of federal fugitives apprehended/cleared:**

a. **Data Definition:** Percent cleared is calculated as the number of cleared fugitives divided by the sum of received fugitives (fugitives with a warrant issued during the fiscal year) and on-hand fugitives (fugitives with active warrants at the start of the fiscal year).

b. **Data Validation and Verification:** Warrant and fugitive data is verified by a random sampling of NCIC records generated by the FBI. The USMS coordinates with district offices to verify that warrants are validated against the signed paper records. The USMS then forwards the validated records back to NCIC.

c. **Data Limitations:** Data is accessible to all districts and updated as new info is collected. There may be a reporting lag.

PERFORMANCE MEASURE TABLE

Decision Unit: Fugitive Apprehension

Performance Report and Performance Plan Targets	FY 2012 Actual	FY 2013 Actual	FY 2014 Actual	FY 2015 Actual	FY 2016 Target	FY 2016 Actual	FY 2017 Target	FY 2018 Target
Performance Measure: Workload								
1. Number of Federal fugitives	N/A	48,525	48,493	49,061	48,540	51,510	49,397	50,869
Performance Measure: Output								
2. Number of assets in inventory	N/A	22,448	21,107	17,564	15,680	15,346	Retired	Retired
a. Cash	N/A	14,704	13,324	10,937	9,500	9,677		
b. Complex Assets	N/A	187	185	224	180	291		
c. All Other Assets	N/A	7,557	7,598	6,403	6,000	5,378		
Performance Measure: Output								
3. Number of assets received**	N/A	N/A	N/A	N/A	13,500	13,537	11,488	11,488
a. Cash	N/A	N/A	N/A	N/A	8,410	7,721	7,200	7,200
b. Complex Assets	N/A	N/A	N/A	N/A	90	183	88	88
c. All Other Assets	N/A	N/A	N/A	N/A	5,000	5,633	4,200	4,200
Performance Measure: Outcome								
4. Number of Federal warrants cleared	N/A	39,267	31,900	32,002	30,144	34,537	30,794	31,711
Performance Measure: Output								
5. Non-Compliant Sex Offender Investigations	N/A	2,009	2,059	1,867	1,786	1,920	1,813	1,840
Performance Measure: Output								
6. Number of assets disposed	N/A	21,983	21,431	19,575	14,500	15,949	12,716	12,716
a. Cash	N/A	14,720	14,367	12,668	9,210	9,508	8,000	8,000
b. Complex Assets	N/A	65	93	115	70	138	96	96
c. All Other Assets	N/A	7,198	6,971	6,792	5,220	6,303	4,620	4,620

N/A = Data unavailable
** Denotes new measure

41

PERFORMANCE MEASURE TABLE

Decision Unit: Fugitive Apprehension

Performance Report and Performance Plan Targets		FY 2012 Actual	FY 2013 Actual	FY 2014 Actual	FY 2015 Actual	FY 2016 Target	FY 2016 Actual	FY 2017 Target	FY 2018 Target
Performance Measure: Output	7. Percent of asset value returned to Fund*	N/A	66%	60%	64%	55%	55%	Retired	Retired
Performance Measure: Output	8. Comparison of value returned to Fund**								
	a. Jewelry, Arts, Antiques & Collectibles	N/A	N/A	N/A	N/A	85%	89%	85%	85%
	b. Real Property	N/A	N/A	N/A	N/A	75%	91%	75%	75%
	c. Conveyances (Vehicles, vessels, and aircraft)	N/A	N/A	N/A	N/A	75%	85%	60%	60%
Performance Measure: Outcome	9. Percent of All Other Assets disposed within procedural time frames*	N/A	57%	60%	57%	60%	55%	Retired	Retired
Performance Measure: Outcome	10. Assets disposed with Procedural Timeframes by Category**								
	a. Real Property	N/A	N/A	N/A	N/A	80%	54%	75%	75%
	b. Conveyances (vehicles, vessels and aircraft)	N/A	N/A	N/A	N/A	80%	75%	85%	85%
Performance Measure: Outcome	11. Number of USMS federal and egregious non-federal fugitives apprehended/cleared	N/A	104,651	105,226	107,001	104,556	106,078	103,468	104,097
Performance Measure: Outcome	12. Number of federal fugitives apprehended/cleared*^	N/A	32,811	30,792	31,202	29,124	32,831	29,638	29,769
	Percent of federal fugitives apprehended/cleared*^	N/A	64%	63%	64%	60%	64%	60%	60%

N/A = **Data unavailable**
* Denotes inclusion in the DOJ Quarterly Status Report
^ Denotes inclusion in the DOJ Annual Performance Plan
** Denotes new measure

3. Performance, Resources, and Strategies

Fugitive Apprehension

One of the challenges facing the fugitive apprehension program is the volume of program responsibility. To achieve the greatest public protection with available resources, the fugitive program focuses on the most egregious federal, state, and local offenders. This requires strategic selection of state and local fugitive cases. The current measures focus on cases in which the USMS has held the primary arresting authority and cases that arguably have a greater impact on public safety, making them a USMS fugitive apprehension priority.

Measure: Number of USMS federal and egregious non-federal fugitives apprehended/cleared
FY 2016 Target: 104,556
FY 2016 Projected: 106,078

Measure: Number and percent of USMS federal fugitives apprehended/cleared
FY 2016 Target: 29,124 / 60%
FY 2016 Actual: 32,831 / 64%

Strategy: Allocate resources effectively to maximize effectiveness in state and local fugitive apprehension

In FY 2016, the USMS leveraged the resources and expertise of federal, state, and local partners to conduct Operation VR12, a national fugitive apprehension initiative focusing on the country's most violent offenders. This six-week operation resulted in the arrest of 8,075 violent fugitives, gang members, and sex offenders. While USMS conducted the operation nationwide, it maximized the impact of deployed resources by identifying and focusing on 12 cities experiencing upticks in violent crime. To further amplify the public safety benefit, investigators targeted recovery of missing children and capture of serial violent fugitives with multiple prior felony arrests for crimes such as murder, attempted murder, robbery, aggravated assault, arson, abduction/kidnapping, weapon offenses, sexual assault, child molestation, and narcotics.

Strategy: Instill program accountability through the implementation of a fugitive case adoption validation process

Implemented in 2012, the Enforcement Operations Standard Operating Procedures (SOP) are designed to enforce a national standard for egregious state and local case adoption among the network of fugitive task forces. Case selection criteria enhance accountability and transparency by establishing a validation process to ensure federal law enforcement only works on cases that meet SOP guidelines. Since 2012, the number of adopted cases that meet these guidelines has steadily increased. Of the nearly 108,000 state and local fugitive cases adopted by the USMS in FY 2016, 92 percent met the national standard.

Strategy: Increase the breadth of foreign fugitive cooperative relationships

The USMS increased its INTERPOL participation by establishing a liaison program to enhance capabilities to identify, locate, and apprehend foreign fugitives. INTERPOL

Bureaus enable police in 190 countries to communicate across a single foreign fugitive who have committed crimes abroad and fled to the United States to avoid detection. This program supplements the resources the USMS already provides to the USNCB by positioning 13 specialized collateral duty investigators in strategic locations throughout the United States.

Strategy: Strengthen USMS investigators' and state and local task force investigators' acumen through innovative training and communication

The USMS increased its ability to assist in investigations of missing children by creating eight collateral duty positions within its Missing Child Unit. The USMS established the Missing Child Unit to oversee and manage its implementation of its enhanced authority under the Justice for Victims of Trafficking Act (P.L. 114-22). These collateral positions are strategically placed nationwide to provide guidance and expertise to USMS investigators and partner law enforcement agencies.

Asset Forfeiture

Asset forfeiture targeting is becoming increasingly complex, creating the need for greater collaboration at all phases of a case. Successful forfeiture requires a cadre of trained individuals with specialized skills and a focus on pre-seizure planning to permit evaluation of the assets seized and the potential value returned to the fund. Continued focus on evaluation of the type of asset seized and effective management of inventory and disposal ensures the highest return to the fund for reinvestment in state and local law enforcement and the community.

Measure: Comparison of Value Returned to the Fund
FY 2016 Target:
Jewelry, Arts, Antiques & Collectibles:	85%
Real Property:	75%
Vehicles:	75%

FY 2016 Actual:
Jewelry, Arts, Antiques & Collectibles:	89%
Real Property:	91%
Vehicles:	85%

Strategy: Increase success by leveraging collaboration between USMS AFP and domestic law enforcement partners to include pre-seizure planning and training

Working collaboratively with participating members of the DOJ AFP, the USMS received and disposed of a wide array of properties to include operating businesses, wine collections, and high-end residential real estate. Two of the more challenging asset types included:

Animals – Enforcement of animal welfare laws is a matter of significant importance to the DOJ. The USMS worked closely with the DOJ Environmental and Natural Resources Division and several federal investigative agencies to implement crime-fighting strategies to break up a number of illegal animal fighting rings. As a result, the USMS provided proper care and treatment for animals when the U.S. Government pursued forfeiture actions to remove them from their abusers. Because the vast majority of seized assets are inanimate, the care and treatment of animals falls outside the scope of routine contracts for asset management and disposal. Therefore, the USMS developed new strategies and partnerships to address these uncommon assets.

Bitcoins – The USMS established an MOU with the Department of Treasury (Treasury) Executive Office for Asset Forfeiture for disposition of forfeited bitcoins emanating from Treasury Forfeiture Fund components. Both DOJ and Treasury recognize the USMS as the government's leader in the sale of virtual currency.

Strategy: Improve the efficiency and effectiveness of AFP lifecycle management to maximize returns supporting victims, law enforcement, and communities

The USMS has worked to ensure the equitable sharing payments program is efficient and effective. Under equitable sharing, proceeds from liquidating assets seized through forfeiture are shared between state and federal law enforcement authorities. The USMS centralized the disbursement of equitable sharing payments, resulting in greater fiscal control and oversight of the expense category.

Strategy: Expand collaboration between AFP and international law enforcement partners

The USMS will increase its effectiveness and recognition within DOJ as the international experts in asset forfeiture activities by maintaining an Investigative Liaison position with the International Unit, Asset Forfeiture and Money Laundering Section, Criminal Division. The USMS will increase its international presence through close collaboration with INTERPOL, the Office of Overseas Prosecutorial Development Assistance and Training, the Office of International Affairs, and the Department of State. Program experts will provide training, assessments, and implementation strategies to foreign governments requesting assistance in the implementation or strengthening of Asset Forfeiture Programs. Training will also be provided to visiting foreign dignitaries as requested.

Non-Compliant Sex Offender Investigations

Working with federal, state, local, and tribal partners, USMS is protecting potential victims from abuse and exploitation by increasing the number of opened investigations related to non-compliant sex offenders. The USMS also coordinates enforcement efforts with USNCB to identify sex offenders engaging in international travel to ensure they are in compliance with their registration.

Measure: Non-compliant Sex Offender Investigations
FY 2016 Target: 1,786
FY 2016 Actual: 1,920

Strategy: Focus on communities lacking specialized sex offender law enforcement resources to include tribal lands and Department of Defense populations

In FY 2016, the USMS executed two projects to improve the ability of communities to track sex offenders: Tribal Outreach and Military Outreach. These projects were designed to strengthen communication and coordination between all levels of law enforcement and those entities that assist with the regulatory process of registration in tribal and DOD populations.

Tribal Outreach: The Tribal Outreach project is designed to improve outreach and coordination with tribes and tribal law enforcement by demonstrating effective tracking of sex offenders on tribal lands. In coordination with the SMART Office and the Office of Tribal Justice, the USMS conducted five tribal working groups and trained attendees from 21 vulnerable tribal communities and more than 50 state and local agencies on the AWA and Sex Offender Registration and Notification Act compliance, planning and conducting sex offender operations, explanation of re-entry notification, and SMART Office resources and grants. The USMS also organized and assisted with five tribal-specific compliance operations, resulting in 190 compliance checks and 11 arrests for AWA violations. This outreach will continue in order to strengthen relationships and increase coordination and communication among tribal, state, local, and federal entities involved in sex offender management in their communities.

Military Outreach: The USMS conducted three outreach initiatives at military installations across the country to improve communication and collaboration related to military sex offender registration investigations. This outreach aimed to ensure the synthesis and coordination of activities between the military sex offender program and state expectations for notification and documentation, especially in scenarios when a service member is convicted of a sex crime and then returns to civilian life. The events were attended by representatives from 37 military units and regional and local law enforcement agencies.

Strategy: Improve the communication and coordination with federal, state, and local partners regarding international traveling sex offenders

As noted previously, the USMS collaborates with the DHS Angel Watch Center as required by IML. IML authorizes the USMS to transmit notification of a sex offender's international travel to the destination country; share information relating to traveling sex offenders with other federal, state, local, and foreign agencies and entities, as appropriate; and receive incoming notifications concerning individuals seeking to enter the United States who have committed offenses of a sexual nature.

In addition to IML-related activities, the USMS partners with the INTERPOL, state, tribal, and territorial sex offender registries, and the Department of State to transmit international notifications on outbound sex offenders. The current program reaches law enforcement in INTERPOL's 190 member countries.

C. Prisoner Security and Transportation

Prisoner Security and Transportation	Direct Positions	Estimated FTE	Amount ($000)
2016 Enacted	1,204	1,037	$259,301
2017 Continuing Resolution	1,204	1,027	$259,647
Adjustments to Base and Technical Adjustments	(305)	(157)	($32,030)
2018 Current Services	899	870	$227,617
2018 Program Increases	7	4	$2,504
2018 Request	906	874	$230,121
Total Change 2017-2018	(298)	(153)	($29,526)

Prisoner Security and Transportation – IT Breakout (of Decision Unit Total)	Direct Positions	Estimated FTE	Amount ($000)
2016 Enacted	21	21	$24,201
2017 Continuing Resolution	21	21	$22,625
Adjustments to Base and Technical Adjustments	0	0	$1,527
2018 Current Services	21	21	$24,152
2018 Program Increases	0	0	$0
2018 Request	21	21	$24,152
Total Change 2017-2018	0	0	$1,527

1. Program Description

The Prisoner Security and Transportation decision unit is complex and multi-layered, both in scope and execution. The USMS oversees all operational detention management matters pertaining to individuals remanded to the custody of the Attorney General. The USMS ensures the secure care and custody of these individuals throughout the judicial process, which includes sustenance, necessary medical care, secure lodging and transportation, evaluating conditions of confinement, and protection of civil rights. Every detainee in USMS custody must be processed by a DUSM or security personnel. This includes processing prisoners in the cellblock (prisoner intake) and securing the cellblock area; transporting prisoners (by ground or air); and locating confinement that provides cost-effective, safe, secure, and humane detention services.

Prisoner Processing and Securing the Cellblock

Prisoner processing includes interviewing the prisoner to gather personal, arrest, prosecution, and medical information; fingerprinting and photographing the prisoner; entering/placing the data and records into an internal electronic database and the prisoner file; and sending the electronic fingerprint information to the FBI's Integrated Automated Fingerprint Identification System (IAFIS). The USMS tracks prisoners primarily in a database from the point a prisoner is received until released from USMS custody or sentenced to the Federal Bureau of Prisons (BOP) for service of sentence.

The cellblock is the secured area for holding prisoners in the courthouse before and after they are scheduled to appear in their court proceedings. Security personnel follow strict safety protocols in the cellblocks to ensure the safety of USMS employees and all members of the judicial process, including prisoners. Prior to entrance into the cellblock, security personnel search prisoners and their belongings to ensure that prisoners and their property are free of contraband. Security personnel are required to be present when cells are unlocked or entered, when prisoners are moved into or out of the cellblock or holding cell areas, when prisoners of the opposite sex are being handled, or when meals are being served. Female and juvenile prisoners must be separated by sight and sound from adult male prisoners within the cellblock. While in the cellblock, security personnel must observe and count the prisoners at regular intervals.

Prisoner Transportation

The USMS is responsible for transporting prisoners to and from judicial proceedings. Producing prisoners for court and detention-related activities requires USMS coordination with the U.S. Courts, Probation and Pretrial Service Offices, the BOP, U.S. Attorneys, and other law enforcement agencies.

Some jails agree to transport prisoners to and from courthouses at specified rates through an Intergovernmental Agreement (IGA) for guard services; other prisoners are transported by USMS operational personnel and contract guards. Security personnel coordinate with jails to prepare prisoners for transport, search prisoners prior to transport, and properly restrain prisoners during transportation.

In addition, the USMS is responsible for transporting prisoners between detention facilities for attorney visits, to and from medical appointments when necessary, and to a designated BOP facility after sentencing. When prisoners are wanted in more than one district for multiple federal violations, the USMS is responsible for transporting prisoners to the requesting district upon completion of the court process in the home district.

Finally, the USMS operates and maintains the fleet of aircraft that comprise the Justice Prisoner and Alien Transportation System (JPATS). JPATS is a revolving fund – total operating costs are reimbursed by its customer agencies, primarily the USMS Federal Prisoner Detention (FPD) appropriation and the BOP. JPATS coordinates movement of the majority of federal prisoners and detainees in the custody of the USMS and the BOP. JPATS also transports Department of Defense, and state and local prisoners on a reimbursable, space-available basis.

Prisoner Confinement and Services

The USMS must ensure sufficient resources are available to house and care for the corresponding detainees. To ensure that federal detainees are being confined securely and humanely and to protect their statutory and constitutional rights, the USMS established the Conditions of Confinement Program. Security personnel conduct annual reviews of all active Intergovernmental Agreement (IGA) facilities. Additionally, detention facility inspections are required before the USMS enters into an IGA with a facility to house prisoners.

The care of federal detainees in private, state, and local facilities, and the costs associated with these efforts are funded from the FPD appropriation. FPD resources are expended from the time a prisoner is brought into USMS custody through termination of the criminal proceeding and/or commitment to BOP. Detention resources provide for detainee housing and subsistence, health care and medical guards, intra-district transportation, JPATS transportation, process improvements, and incidental costs associated with prisoner housing and transportation such as prisoner meals while in transit and prisoner clothing.

2. Performance and Resource Tables

PERFORMANCE AND RESOURCES TABLE

Decision Unit: Prisoner Security and Transportation

RESOURCES ($ in thousands)	Target FY 2016		Actual FY 2016		Target FY 2017		Changes — Current Services Adjustments and FY 2018 Program Changes		Requested (Total) FY 2018 Request	
	FTE	Amount	FTE	Amount	FTE	Amount	FTE	Amount	FTE	Amount
Total Costs and FTE (reimbursable FTE are included, but reimbursable costs are bracketed and not included in the total)	1,027	$259,301 [$0]	1,037	$264,482 [$2,700]	1,027	$259,647 [$896]	(153)	($29,526) [$0]	874	$230,121 [$896]

TYPE	PERFORMANCE	Target FY 2016		Actual FY 2016		Target FY 2017		Changes — Current Services Adjustments and FY 2018 Program Changes		Requested (Total) FY 2018 Request	
		FTE	Amount	FTE	Amount	FTE	Amount	FTE	Amount	FTE	Amount
Program Activity		1,027	$259,301 [$0]	1,037	$264,482 [$2,700]	1,027	$259,647 [$896]	(153)	($29,526) [$0]	874	$230,121 [$896]
Performance Measure: Workload	1. Average daily prisoner population		52,644		51,400		53,214		0		53,214
Performance Measure: Outcome	2. Percent of monitoring reviews completed for active IGAs		98%		100%		98%		0%		98%
Performance Measure: Outcome	3. Total prisoner productions		820,800		836,522		833,047		0		833,047
Performance Measure: Outcome	4. Average detention cost (housing, medical and in-district transportation)*,**		$86.46		$86.83		$88.05		$0.00		$88.05

* Denotes inclusion in the DCJ Quarterly Status Report
** Reported as part of the USMS Federal Prisoner Detention Appropriation

50

Data Definition, Validation, Verification, and Limitations:

Performance Measures – Workload

1. Average Daily Prisoner Population:

a) **Data Definition:** Average Daily Prisoner Population is calculated on a per capita, per day basis.

b) **Data Validation and Verification:** Data is maintained by the Justice Detainee Information System (JDIS). Monthly data from JDIS relating to paid detention beds is verified each month by completing a comparison, by district, between obligation data being reported out of UFMS and prisoner program data reported from JDIS.

c) **Data Limitations:** Limited by the timely entry of prisoner data into JDIS.

Performance Measures – Outputs, Efficiencies, and Outcomes

2. Percent of Monitoring reviews completed for active IGAs:

a) **Data Definition:** Percentage of IGA facilities used by the USMS to house prisoners with a completed monitoring review.

b) **Data Validation and Verification:** Each year USMS personnel run reports comparing the facilities that should be inspected to those that were inspected.

c) **Data Limitations:** Limited by the timely entry of monitoring review results and identifying the appropriate facilities.

3. Total Prisoner Productions:

a) **Data Definition:** Total prisoners produced data combines both the USMS District counts and DC Superior Court counts, and includes the number of times prisoners are produced for judicial proceedings, meetings with attorneys, or transported for medical care, between offices and between detention facilities.

b) **Data Validation and Verification:** USMS District data is maintained by JDIS. DC Superior Court data is maintained by a locally-managed database and is updated daily. DC Superior Court will be transitioning to JDIS in the near future.

c) **Data Limitations:** Limited by the timely entry of prisoner data into JDIS and DC Superior Court's database, as appropriate. For DC Superior Court, more than 95% of prisoner productions are entered into the system on the same day they occur.

4. Average Detention Cost (Housing, Medical, and In-District Transportation):

a) **Data Definition:** Total detention costs represent the aggregation of paid jail costs and health care costs on a per capita, per day basis.

b) Data Validation and Verification: Data reported is validated and verified against monthly reports describing district-level jail utilization and housing costs prepared by the USMS. In accordance with generally accepted accounting principles, the USMS routinely monitors its financial data for new obligations and de-obligations.

c) Data Limitations: Maintaining prisoner movement data is a labor-intensive process. The reliability of the reported data is often compromised by time lags between the actual movement of prisoners and data entry of those events into JDIS. Accordingly, it is often necessary to delay reporting of official statistics several weeks to ensure that prisoner movement records have been properly updated. Data reported reflect the anticipated cost of services provided to USMS prisoners. In the event that the actual cost is different from the anticipated cost, additional funds may need to be obligated or obligated funds, de-obligated. Due to the time lag between the rendering of services and the payment of invoices, several weeks may lapse before the actual cost of health care services provided to an individual prisoner can be determined.

52

PERFORMANCE MEASURE TABLE

Decision Unit: Prisoner Security and Transportation

Performance Report and Performance Plan Targets	FY 2012 Actual	FY 2013 Actual	FY 2014 Actual	FY 2015 Actual	FY 2016 Target	FY 2016 Actual	FY 2017 Target	FY 2018 Target
Performance Measure: Workload								
1. Average daily prisoner population	N/A	59,542	55,420	55,420	52,644	51,400	53,214	53,214
Performance Measure: Outcome								
2. Percent of monitoring reviews completed for active IGAs		Established Baseline	94%	94%	98%	100%	98%	98%
Performance Measure: Outcome								
3. Total prisoner productions	N/A	1,018,693	940,636	940,636	820,800	836,522	833,047	833,047
Performance Measure: Outcome								
4. Average detention cost (housing, medical, and in-district transportation)*,**	N/A	$80.33	$82.92	$82.92	$86.46	$86.83	$88.05	$88.05

N/A = Data unavailable

* Denotes inclusion in the DOJ Quarterly Status Report

** Reported also as part of the USMS Federal Prisoner Detention Appropriation

3. Performance, Resources, and Strategies

The USMS assures the integrity of the federal judicial system by maintaining the custody, protection, and security of prisoners and ensuring that criminal defendants appear for judicial proceedings. Efficient management of detention resources necessitates that the USMS continuously analyze the courts' need for prisoners in relation to detention facility location and cost. This evaluation results in strategic movement of prisoners to various detention facilities as their cases progress. Prisoners are moved to closer facilities when they are more often needed to appear for court (for example, pretrial prisoners). Prisoners are moved to more distant facilities (which are often less costly) as their need to appear in court decreases. The USMS annually reviews every detention facility it utilizes to ensure conditions of confinement are humane and provide adequate security.

Measure: Average Detention Cost
FY 2016 Target: $86.46
FY 2016 Actual: $86.83
FY 2018 Projected: $88.05

Strategy: Develop defined business practices with BOP to better track, manage, and utilize federal detention space within BOP

> Improving detention contract management: The USMS improved detention contractor performance monitoring by establishing an on-site monitoring program staffed by full-time professional Detention Contract Administrators in two districts where USMS uses private detention facilities to house prisoners. The Detention Contract Monitoring Program will ensure Contracting Officer's Representatives are better trained in detention matters, improving contract monitoring and service.

> Improving conditions of confinement: The USMS revised the Federal Performance Based Detention Standards to incorporate the DOJ Guiding Principles outlined in "Report and Recommendations Concerning the Use of Restrictive Housing." This revision incorporates guiding principles applicable to a pre-trial private detention environment which exceed the standards previously codified in the Standards. The revised Standards addressed a Presidential Memorandum and improved conditions of confinement for prisoners in restrictive housing.

Strategy: Transition to the Justice Automated Booking System

> To facilitate the transition to the Justice Automated Booking System, the USMS developed a prototype of an electronic signature pad and electronic versions of key property and medical release paper forms that detention personnel can sign and store digitally. These electronic versions will replace multi-part paper forms and simplify sharing information as defendants move through USMS jurisdictions to BOP facilities. Additionally, the USMS will save $27,000 annually by eliminating printing, storing, and archiving costs of paper forms.

Strategy: Assess the feasibility of establishing regional post-sentencing receiving centers

The USMS initiated a pilot project at the Robert A. Deyton Detention Facility in the Northern District of Georgia to test the viability of establishing Regional Receiving Centers as staging areas for sentenced prisoners pending movement to their designated BOP facilities. The pilot project, expected to conclude by June 2017, serves as a proof of concept, enabling the USMS to assess staffing needs, improve the sentence-to-commitment workflow, and identify best practices and lessons learned. Regional Receiving Centers will improve availability of detention beds in court cities, and enable the USMS to adjust detention capacity to meet changing demands.

Strategy: Assess the feasibility and cost-effectiveness of implementing strategically sourced detention services

USMS established a Restraint Blanket Purchase Agreement (BPA) with an associated directive and SOPs to allow districts to order USMS-approved restraining devices at a competitive price using a standard procurement process. The competitive national award of the common USMS Restraint BPA will result in cost savings by eliminating unnecessary BPAs; improving inventory control, reporting, and budget forecasting; and providing uniform restraint devices across all districts.

Strategy: Automate the IGA review process to increase standardization, meet applicable regulations and laws, and target areas for improvement

The USMS issued the 2016 Detention Services Price Analysis Guide for detention and correctional services contracts and IGAs to assist organizations in performing pre-negotiation price analysis when determining reasonableness of price for services, forecasting budgetary estimates, and conducting market research. The guide, which has generated $204.3 million in cost savings since its implementation in 2007, will continue to help the USMS negotiate fair and reasonable per diem rates at IGA facilities.

Strategy: Develop cost effective solutions for the care of chronically ill USMS prisoners

The USMS continued to refine the requirements of the National Managed Care Contract Statement of Work. These refinements will reduce pharmacy costs by re-establishing a pharmacy program with medication discounts and generic medication substitutions and streamline prisoner medical bill payments by ensuring prisoner medical claim processing and payments comply with the Medicare payment standards established by 18 U.S.C. 4006. The USMS will also ensure contract requirements are consistent with the new USMS data management system.

D. Protection of Witnesses

Protection of Witnesses	Direct Positions	Estimated FTE	Amount ($000)
2016 Enacted	207	178	$36,734
2017 Continuing Resolution	207	146	$36,647
Adjustments to Base and Technical Adjustments	63	115	$18,224
2018 Current Services	270	261	$54,871
2018 Program Increases	2	1	$668
2018 Request	272	262	$55,539
Total Change 2017-2018	65	116	$18,892

Protection of Witnesses – IT Breakout (of Decision Unit Total)	Direct Positions	Estimated FTE	Amount ($000)
2016 Enacted	3	3	$3,457
2017 Continuing Resolution	3	3	$3,232
Adjustments to Base and Technical Adjustments	0	0	$218
2018 Current Services	3	3	$3,450
2018 Program Increases	0	0	$0
2018 Request	3	3	$3,450
Total Change 2017-2018	0	0	$218

1. Program Description

The Witness Security Program (WSP) provides protection for government witnesses whose lives are threatened as a result of their testimony against drug traffickers, terrorists, organized crime members, and other major criminals. The program also provides physical security during trial proceedings, assistance to create new identities, and relocation of witnesses and their families after trial. The successful operation of the WSP is widely recognized as providing a unique and valuable tool in the government's war against organized crime, drug cartels, violent criminal gangs, and terrorist groups.

Three DOJ components work collaboratively to administer the WSP. The Criminal Division's Office of Enforcement Operations authorizes the entry of witnesses into the program. The BOP protects witnesses incarcerated in federal prison facilities. The USMS protects civilian witnesses and their families, providing protection, relocation, re-identification, and assistance with housing, medical care, job training, and employment until they become self-sufficient.

2. Performance and Resource Tables

PERFORMANCE AND RESOURCES TABLE										

Decision Unit: Protection of Witnesses

RESOURCES ($ in thousands)	Target FY 2016		Actual FY 2016		Target FY 2017		Changes — Current Services Adjustments and FY 2018 Program Changes		Requested (Total) FY 2018 Request	
	FTE	Amount	FTE	Amount	FTE	Amount	FTE	Amount	FTE	Amount
Total Costs and FTE (Reimbursable: FTE are included, but costs are bracketed and not included in totals)	147	$36,734 [$782]	179	$37,231 [$318]	147	$36,647 [$661]	116	$18,892 [$0]	263	$55,539 [$661]
TYPE — PERFORMANCE	147	$36,734 [$782]	179	$37,231 [$318]	147	$36,647 [$661]	116	$18,892 [$0]	263	$55,539 [$661]
Program Activity Performance Measure: Workload — 1. Total number of witness security program participants		18,760		18,751		18,830		0		18,830
Performance Measure: Output — 2. Protection services required/provided for witnesses (includes court productions)		2,560		2,455		2,550		0		2,550
Performance Measure: Outcome — 3. Security breaches mitigated*		138		133		125		0		125

* Denotes inclusion in the DOJ Quarterly Status Report

Data Definition, Validation, Verification, and Limitations:

Performance Measures – Workload

1. **Total number of witness security program participants:**

    a. **Data Definition:** The total number of program participants, including immediate family members.

    b. **Data Validation and Verification:** Case managers ensure the accuracy of data submitted to headquarters.

    c. **Data Limitations:** Case management provides data on a monthly basis.

Performance Measures – Outputs, Efficiencies, and Outcomes

2. **Protective services required/provided for witnesses (includes court productions):**

    a. **Data Definition:** Total number of witness productions, prisoner witness transports, prisoner witness family visits, preliminary interviews, temporary relocations, documentation initiations, documentation services (delivery-other), and breach investigations.

    b. **Data Validation and Verification:** Regional managers ensure the accuracy of data submitted to headquarters.

    c. **Data Limitations:** Witness Security Division (WSD) regions provide data to headquarters on a monthly basis.

3. **Security breaches mitigated:**

    a. **Data Definition:** An action taken to mitigate a reported or detected event capable of compromising a protected witness' identity, location or general security.

    b. **Data Validation and Verification:** Validation occurs when the actions taken have been documented, reviewed, and approved. Verification occurs when internal audits are conducted to identify the efficiency and effectiveness of the actions taken.

    c. **Data Limitations:** The total number of security breaches is dependent upon the number of breaches reported or detected. Actions to mitigate the security breaches only occur when security breaches are detected or reported. A substantial number of security breaches are believed to be unreported or undetected.

PERFORMANCE MEASURE TABLE

Decision Unit: Protection of Witnesses

Performance Report and Performance Plan Targets	FY 2012	FY 2013	FY 2014	FY 2015	FY 2016		FY 2017	FY 2018
	Actual	Actual	Actual	Actual	Target	Actual	Target	Target
Performance Measure: Workload 1. Total number of witness security program participants	N/A	18,516	18,574	18,685	18,760	18,751	18,830	18,830
Performance Measure: Output 2. Protective services required/provided for witnesses (includes court productions)	N/A	3,334	3,629	2,477	2,560	2,455	2,550	2,550
Performance Measure: Outcome 3. Security breaches mitigated*	N/A	256	210	152	138	133	125	125

* Denotes inclusion in the DOJ Quarterly Status Report

59

3. Performance, Resources, and Strategies

The funding is necessary to ensure that critical protective services are provided to protected witnesses testifying in direct support of significant DOJ prosecutorial efforts against organized crime, international drug trafficking organizations, violent street gangs, and international terrorist groups. The USMS continues to examine WSP methodologies to ensure that effective protection and security services are provided to protected witnesses and authorized participants while also exercising cost efficiencies.

Measure: Security Breaches Mitigated
FY 2016 Target: 138
FY 2016 Actual: 133

Strategy: Define levels of service, potential growth, and impact to resources

Streamlining administrative and operational planning: Two key objectives of protection involve the safe movement of witnesses and their appearance in court. During FY 2016, the USMS modified its application management system to centralize and standardize administrative and operational planning. This new tool streamlined the approval and notification functions, eliminating cumbersome, inconsistent, manual processes. It enables management to track resources, personnel, and costs by record, date, or location. The application improves witness security business processes by ensuring operational plans are complete, consistent, and receive appropriate approvals. Financial controls verify that expenses are categorized correctly and in compliance with USMS policies related to financial and workload reports.

Continuing strategic risk mitigation: In FY 2016, USMS successfully completed the first part of a two-phase project to develop and use risk assessment tools for more effective program management. This project shifts decision-making from a manual approach to an enhanced operational decision-making process that enables improved decision logic. Phase I confirmed the critical decision elements and the creation of a prototype tool to assess risk and enhance the retention of witnesses in the protection program. In Phase II, the prototype tool will evolve into an enterprise-wide application that incorporates core business processes for witness protection of witnesses, with an application that leverages geospatial capabilities to support relocation-based decisions. These tools will strengthen the USMS's ability to assess and manage risk while supporting the development of risk-based decision logic and informed management plans with the ultimate intent of improving retention.

E. Tactical Operations

Tactical Operations	Direct Positions	Estimated FTE	Amount ($000)
2016 Enacted	177	174	$45,592
2017 President's Budget	177	174	$47,496
Adjustments to Base and Technical Adjustments	(4)	(6)	$1,814
2018 Current Services	173	168	$49,310
2018 Program Increases	2	1	$5,617
2018 Request	175	169	$54,927
Total Change 2017-2018	(2)	(5)	$7,431

Tactical Operations – IT Breakout (of Decision Unit Total)	Direct Positions	Estimated FTE	Amount ($000)
2016 Enacted	3	3	$3,457
2017 President's Budget	3	3	$3,232
Adjustments to Base and Technical Adjustments	0	0	$218
2018 Current Services	3	3	$3,450
2018 Program Increases	0	0	$0
2018 Request	3	3	$3,450
Total Change 2017-2018	0	0	$218

1. Program Description

The Tactical Operations decision unit includes special operations and emergency management.

Special Operations

The Special Operations Group (SOG) supports the DOJ and other government agencies with a highly-trained, rapidly deployable force of law enforcement officers for tactical response. Based at the Special Operations Group Tactical Center (SOGTC) in Camp Beauregard, Louisiana, SOG is a unit of DUSMs who meet high qualification standards and complete rigorous training in a variety of specialties. SOG supports all U.S. judicial districts by assisting with high-risk, sensitive law enforcement operations including protective details, national emergencies, civil disturbances, and national disasters. Military, federal, state, local, and foreign law enforcement groups often call upon SOG for training due to the extensive training of its members in various tactical specialties.

SOG also oversees the Operational Medical Support Unit (OMSU), which is composed of both SOG Medics and Collateral Duty DUSM Medics. The OMSU program manages, trains, and equips USMS DUSMs who possess a current Emergency Medical Technician (EMT) or EMT-Paramedic certification.

Emergency Management and Response

All USMS operational missions that fall under emergency management and response are coordinated through the USMS Communications Center and the Emergency Operations Center (EOC). The Communications Center operates around the clock to ensure interagency and intra-agency flow of communication. It provides informational assistance to DUSMs in the field who are tracking fugitives, developing leads, and confirming warrants. It also receives, tracks, and disseminates all significant incidents and classified information relevant to the USMS.

The EOC is activated during emergency incidents that require a coordinated agency-wide response, including responses under the federal government's National Response Framework. The EOC is a critical element to ensure coordination and oversight of USMS deployments during emergencies, particularly when other government agencies are also involved.

In addition to the EOC, emergency management officials maintain the Continuity of Operations (COOP) plan for the USMS Headquarters and coordinate the COOP plans of all 94 districts in accordance with Federal Continuity Directives and DOJ Order 1900.8.

The USMS also oversees Incident Management Teams (IMTs) that are trained under the principles and doctrines of the National Incident Management System and the Incident Command System, in accordance with Homeland Security Presidential Directive 5. These teams deploy in support of USMS operations when an incident or event exceeds the capabilities of the district's or division's resources or when multiple districts or divisions are affected.

2. Performance and Resource Tables

PERFORMANCE AND RESOURCES TABLE

Decision Unit: Tactical Operations

RESOURCES ($ in thousands)		Target FY 2016		Actual FY 2016		Target FY 2017		Changes Current Services Adjustments and FY 2018 Program Changes		Requested (Total) FY 2018 Request	
		FTE	Amount	FTE	Amount	FTE	Amount	FTE	Amount	FTE	Amount
Total Costs and FTE (Reimbursable: FTE are included, but costs are bracketed and not included in totals)		211	$45,592 [$12,197]	187	$46,817 [$10,052]	211	$47,496 [$11,515]	(5)	$7,431 [$0]	206	$54,927 [$11,515]
TYPE	**PERFORMANCE**	FY 2016		FY 2016		FY 2017		Current Services Adjustments and FY 2018 Program Changes		FY 2018 Request	
		FTE	Amount	FTE	Amount	FTE	Amount	FTE	Amount	FTE	Amount
Program Activity		211	$45,592 [$12,197]	187	$46,817 [$10,052]	211	$47,496 [$11,515]	(5)	$7,431 [$0]	206	$54,927 [$12,197]
Performance Measure: Output	1. Number of high-threat and emergency situations supported through special operations and assignments		59		111		Retired		Retired		Retired
Performance Measure: Output	2. Number of special operational hours dedicated to high-threat and emergency situations.		49,679		31,040		43,412		0		43,412

N/A = Data unavailable

63

Data Definition, Validation, Verification, and Limitations:

Performance Measures – Outputs, Efficiencies, and Outcomes

1. **Number of high-threat and emergency situations supported through special operations and assignments – Retired:** *Transition to number of special operation hours dedicated to high-threat and emergency situations*

   a. **Data Definition:** This represents the number of times a special occurrence or event happened where special operations and assignment resources and/or staff were deployed in response.

   b. **Data Validation:** Deployments are validated against financial and special assignment data.

   c. **Data Limitation:** Deployments are tracked via a manual process.

2. **Number of special operation hours dedicated to high-threat and emergency situations – New (see note above)**

   a. **Data Definition:** The number of hours USMS SOG members expended in response to a high threat or emergency event. Success is defined as actuals below the target. Target represents maximum performance.

   b. **Data Validation:** Hours are validated against financial and special assignment data.

   Data Limitation: Hours are tracked via a manual process.

PERFORMANCE MEASURE TABLE

Decision Unit: Tactical Operations

Performance Report and Performance Plan Targets	FY 2012	FY 2013	FY 2014	FY 2015	FY 2016		FY 2017	FY 2018
	Actual	Actual	Actual	Actual	Target	Actual	Target	Target
Performance Measure: Output	1. Number of high-threat and emergency situations supported through special operations and assignments	52	75	113	120	59	111	Retired	Retired
Performance Measure: Output	2. Number of special operational hours dedicated to high-threat and emergency situations.	N/A	N/A	N/A	N/A	49,679	31,040	43,412	43,412

65

3. Performance, Resources, and Strategies

The USMS provides effective assistance to all levels of government during emergencies, disasters, and times of heightened law enforcement requirements. The USMS deploys personnel and equipment in response to extraordinary district requirements, ensuring adequate resources are provided to maintain the integrity of the judicial process. The USMS is committed to:

- improving its capability to deploy personnel and equipment in response to terrorist acts, natural disasters, and other external missions directed by the Attorney General;

- maintaining operational readiness for efficient movement of people and equipment; and

- coordinating communication between the Strategic National Stockpile Security Operations Unit and the Centers for Disease Control and Prevention to ensure adequate dissemination of intelligence information to thwart or respond to terrorist activities.

Measure: Number of special operational hours dedicated to high-threat and emergency situations
FY 2016 Target: 49,679
FY 2016 Actual: 31,040

Strategy: Expand the USMS' medical response capability and ensure adequate medical support for the mission

Providing medic support to USMS missions: OMSU medics are the USMS's key provider of medical support to district and national judicial missions. The effectiveness of the OMSU program in providing immediate medical support during missions has generated an increase in the number of requests for OMSU medics. To address this increased need, the USMS expanded its medical response capability, by including DUSMs who are currently certified as EMTs. The USMS has developed a long-term budget strategy to guarantee adequate funding to conduct mandatory specialty and re-certification training for these positions.

Training to deal with active threats: The USMS provided training to HQ operational and administrative employees on Active Shooter/Active Threat trauma medicine. This training is vital in preparing USMS HQ employees for a variety of situations. For this training, operational employees benefited from an updated Deputy Trauma Curriculum that included revised tactical guidelines and modernized videos. All OMSU medics and 15 SOG medics are certified to teach the updated curriculum. Additionally, OMSU DUSM medics instructed medical training for stand-alone Deputy Trauma Courses in districts and divisions as well as for Deputy Trauma Courses in conjunction with HRFA courses.

Deploying the Automatic Electronic Defibrillator (AED) Program: AEDs provide first responders with an effective means of treating and reversing cardiac arrest within minutes. The USMS provides AED training to its employees and court staff to render critical, life-saving measures to employees and members of the public; only those who complete the training are authorized to use them. The USMS AED program complies with the recognized standards of the American Heart Association certification policy. To increase program effectiveness, the USMS developed new AED policy requirements and operating procedures to ensure consistency across all districts and divisions, sourced new equipment suppliers, and established a cyclical replacement plan for obsolete AED units. Additionally, the USMS revised training materials to include more stringent standards to meet certification requirements and certified 32 instructors to train personnel.

Strategy: Ensure sustainable tactical communication and network functionality and delivery of services

Delivering tactical communications support: The USMS routinely deploys communications networks to further various agency missions and in support of other federal, state, and local law enforcement efforts. In FY 2016, the USMS deployed tactical communications support for special missions such as an Amber Alert, a non-profit sporting event that required the assistance of law enforcement, the Republican and Democratic National Conventions, a courthouse protest of more than 1,000 people, and a large-scale fugitive round-up. For these special missions, the USMS deployed satellite phones, MSATs, video surveillance equipment, radios programmed to federal law enforcement channels, desktop base station radios, and a Mobile Command Center. The USMS provided on-the-spot equipment training to local law enforcement personnel detailed to the missions.

Providing reliable radio communications at U.S. Court facilities: The USMS provides reliable, encrypted radio communication capabilities in United States Court facilities and manages the courthouse tactical communications systems for DUSMs, CSOs, and courthouse personnel. In FY 2016, the USMS replaced seven aging radio repeater systems at U.S. Courthouses and installed six new repeaters at sites that previously relied on handheld radios for communications. These repeaters improved radio coverage at courthouses, and the safety of the CSOs and court staff. The USMS deployed 150 new portable radios to replace obsolete equipment, and refurbished and reissued approximately 200 radios. These initiatives will help to ensure courthouse communications systems continue to function optimally and substantially save further expenditures.

Updating and expanding radio transmissions: Through its Marshals Service Communication Application Network, the USMS provides Over The Air Re-Key (OTAR) and command-and-control functionality to CSOs and DUSM radios at U.S. Court facilities and radio systems nationally. This program uses a consolidated network to transmit radio information to U.S. District Courthouses, resulting in a significant cost savings as traditionally network connections between sites would require a separate Internet or telephone circuit. In FY 2016, the USMS improved the reliability of OTAR and other system functionality and made significant progress in migrating away from legacy equipment by continuing to update the Marshals Service Communication Application Network. Additionally, in FY 2016, new OTAR capability was provided to additional sites across the country, expanding this capability to all USMS and CSO users.

V. Program Increases by Item

Item Name: **Deputy U.S. Marshals Life and Safety**

Budget Decision Unit(s): Judicial and Courthouse Security
Fugitive Apprehension
Prisoner Security and Transportation
Protection of Witnesses
Tactical Operations

Organizational Program: Cyclical Equipment Replacement

Program Increase: Positions <u>0</u> Agt/Atty <u>0</u> FTE <u>0</u> Dollars <u>$12,000,000</u>

Description of Item

The USMS requests **$12,000,000** for the cyclical replacement of body armor, radios, vehicles, surveillance equipment, as well as Special Operations Group (SOG) selection, specialty and mandatory recertification and equipment. This funding would enable the USMS to institutionalize the replacement cycle so that equipment is replaced on a regular annual basis.

Justification

The USMS received approximately 1,000 new positions between 2009 and 2010. The positions came with modular costs to include vehicles, radios, computer and protective equipment. In subsequent years, the USMS never received full funding for these positions. As a result, rising mandatory costs, such as salary/benefits and rent have eroded base funding for equipment associated with these new hires. To sustain the positions, the USMS lost its flexibility to fund cyclical replacement needs going forward. The USMS will continue to implement cost-cutting efforts in all areas wherever possible.

LAND MOBILE RADIOS (LMR) – $2,683,000

Land mobile radios are vital for operational communications within the USMS and are critical in all officer safety scenarios. The USMS issues dual band equipment that is interoperable with all other federal components, as well as state and local law enforcement partners and agencies throughout the country.

The request would fund a five-year replacement cycle to ensure that deputies have reliable and encrypted communications, and that the USMS stays abreast of the latest technology. Maintaining a reliable replacement cycle ensures that the equipment stays within the manufacturer's five-year serviceable schedule. Retaining models past five years is costly because parts may not be available. In the worst case, manufacturers stop producing spare parts for models outside the 10-year production run.

The USMS requests **$2,683,000** to upgrade outdated LMR equipment on a five-year schedule. Each deputy is issued a handheld radio at a cost of $8,400 each and accessories such as batteries, antennas, and earpieces are $900 per deputy. Every vehicle is equipped with a mobile radio at a cost of approximately $9,400 each to include installation.

Item	Quantity	Unit Cost	Total Cost	Replacement Cycle	Annual Replacement Cost
Handheld radios	735	$8,400	$6,174,000	5 years	$1,235,000
Handheld radio accessories	735	$900	$661,500	5 years	$132,000
Mobile radios, access and install	700	$9,400	$6,580,600	5 years	$1,316,000
Total					**$2,683,000**

Effective and encrypted tactical communications capabilities are essential to the safety of DUSMs during the performance of their duties. Funding this initiative would ensure that the LMR program within the USMS stays at the forefront of tactical communications technology and is able to provide operational personnel with the best possible communications solution during the execution of dangerous missions.

The request would allow the USMS to purchase 147 handheld radios and 140 mobile radios each year. The USMS assumes a replacement cycle of five years.

SPECIAL OPERATIONS GROUP (SOG) SELECTION, SPECIALTY AND MANDATORY RECERTIFICATION TRAINING – $2,263,000

The USMS requests **$2,263,000** to establish base funding to support annual, recurring requirements for the SOG Selection Course, Specialty Training, and Mandatory Recertification Training (MRT) as well as Law Enforcement Safety Training Program (LESTP) initiatives and related equipment.

Item	Unit Cost	Quantity	FY 2018 Request
Mandatory Recertification Training (MRT)	$500,000	2	$1,000,000
Specialty Training Recertification	$287,000	1	$287,000
SOG Selection Course	$300,000	1	$300,000
Operational, Training and Protective Equip.	$540,000	1	$540,000
Specialty Training and Operational Vehicles	$135,475	1	$136,000
Total			**$2,263,000**

The USMS SOG is a highly trained tactical unit that conducts specialty operations both within and outside the United States. SOG is deployed to support the DOJ and the USMS operations, which span the range of federal law enforcement missions. SOG's specialty operations support fugitive apprehension, violent sex offender targeted missions, terrorist trials, high-threat prisoner movements, witness security operations, national emergencies, and other missions as ordered by the U.S. Attorney General. Other missions include, but are not limited to, civil disorders, protection of at-risk health facilities and staff, large scale seizures, actions against anti-government and militia groups, and stability and reconstruction efforts. SOG support occurs when a situation is beyond the capability of USMS districts or divisions.

SOG members must maintain the necessary skills to provide tactical support to the USMS and DOJ. The USMS complies with the National Tactical Officers Association (NTOA) training standard of 192 training hours annually per SOG member. It is imperative that SOG members are properly trained to handle the most complex and high-risk missions. A well-trained tactical unit increases officer safety and maximizes efficiency when executing high-risk operations.

Membership in SOG is voluntary. DUSMs interested in joining must submit a comprehensive application package which is competitively graded and scored. Once selected to attend training, candidates undergo a physically rigorous and mentally challenging SOG Selection Course. SOG Selection is a 30-day course where DUSMs are trained in all aspects of SOG equipment, tactics, and SOG standard operating procedures. Each applicant is evaluated in various critical skills to ensure they meet the higher standards of SOG. The course tests DUSMs under physical and mental stress to simulate real world operations in austere environments. SOG Selection courses begin with 30 to 50 candidates, depending on the number of qualified applicants. About 30% of the candidates successfully complete the training and become members of the unit. Failure to complete the course is usually attributed to failure to meet minimum firearms qualification scores, injuries, or voluntarily leaving training for personal reasons. Tenure in SOG varies greatly, from one year to 25 years. As the number of SOG members diminishes, the USMS must conduct annual SOG Selection Training to maintain a force that can manage multiple, simultaneous missions. DUSMs who complete the SOG Selection Course must also be fully equipped and trained in additional specialty areas.

The USMS SOG participated in the Rule of Law, Stability and Reconstruction Programs in Iraq and Afghanistan through reimbursable agreements with DOS and DOD from 2004 through 2014. By enhancing judicial security in these countries, SOGs efforts allowed fair and transparent court processes. The USMS relied on this funding to support USMS SOG training and equipment; however, the SOG mission in Iraq ended in 2011 and the SOG mission in Afghanistan was terminated in September 2014. The requested increase is the minimum required to maintain operational readiness now that the USMS no longer receives DOS and DOD funding.

The USMS has no dedicated base funding to support the requirements for the SOG Selection Course and related equipment; MRT; Specialty Training and recertification; operational training and protective equipment; and operational vehicles. SOG training and equipment costs are separate from the normal cost module for new positions. Funding for training includes travel, per diem, food, contractor administrative support, instructor overtime, and training supplies including ammunition and targets. Funding for equipment includes personal protective equipment, uniforms, firearms, operational ammunition, night vision devices, breaching equipment, communication equipment, and armored vehicles.

The USMS trains SOG deputies at the Special Operations Group Tactical Center (SOGTC), within the confines of Camp Beauregard, the Louisiana Army National Guard (LANG) base in Pineville, Louisiana. The USMS leases four separate facilities from LANG totaling approximately 120,000 square feet on 200 acres of property. SOG is the only tactical unit within the USMS. Through its 85 collateral SOG members and its 75 Operational Medical Support Unit Deputy Medics, the USMS provides immediate regional support for daily operations across the country. SOG members participate in fugitive intensive strike teams targeting violent federal and state fugitives, to include sex offenders. These tactically-trained Deputies help reduce the number of violent felons on the street correlating to the reduction of trafficking, the use of illegal drugs, and the diversion of licit drugs. SOG operations directly support initiatives to reduce violent crime, take guns off the street and target violent criminal gangs.

The specialized areas of instruction during SOG training include sniper/observer, explosive and manual breaching, evasive driving, waterborne operations, less-lethal chemical and impact munitions and weaponry, tactical medicine, high angle insertion, weapons of mass destruction, various types of instructor training, civil disturbance, and officer safety training among others. SOG trains several times a year to comply with national standards for training of tactical and medical personnel.

The core of the SOG workforce comprises highly trained criminal investigators who are activated and respond to SOG missions when necessary. When not on a SOG deployment, these criminal investigators are assigned full-time to USMS districts across the nation, where they perform their normal duties as DUSMs. SOG's pool of well-trained, instructor-certified DUSMs provides district and regional training to mitigate risk to DUSMs in the field. This includes, but is not limited to, medical training, advanced firearms training and qualification, Active Shooter/Active Threat training, tactical entry training and Taser certification.

The USMS is specifically sought after to conduct national security operations on behalf of various U.S. Government entities due to its unequaled authority and jurisdiction. The USMS SOG is often chosen for these national security operations due to the sensitive, covert nature of these missions, which require personnel with elevated security clearances and specific training, equipment and tactical assets. These programs, which directly affect the ability to prevent terrorism and promote the Nation's security consistent with the rule of law, will be at risk if this initiative is not properly funded to train and equip its personnel.

BODY ARMOR – $1,330,000

The USMS currently issues every operational employee a body armor kit that consists of an Urban Assault Vest (UAV), Undercover Vest (UC), and Multi-Mission Armor Carrier (MMAC) plate carrier. Each body armor kit is precisely measured to fit a specific individual and cannot be re-used by others. The USMS purchased and issued the majority of the vests in 2012. The USMS replaces body armor every five years, which is also the length of the manufacturer's warranty.

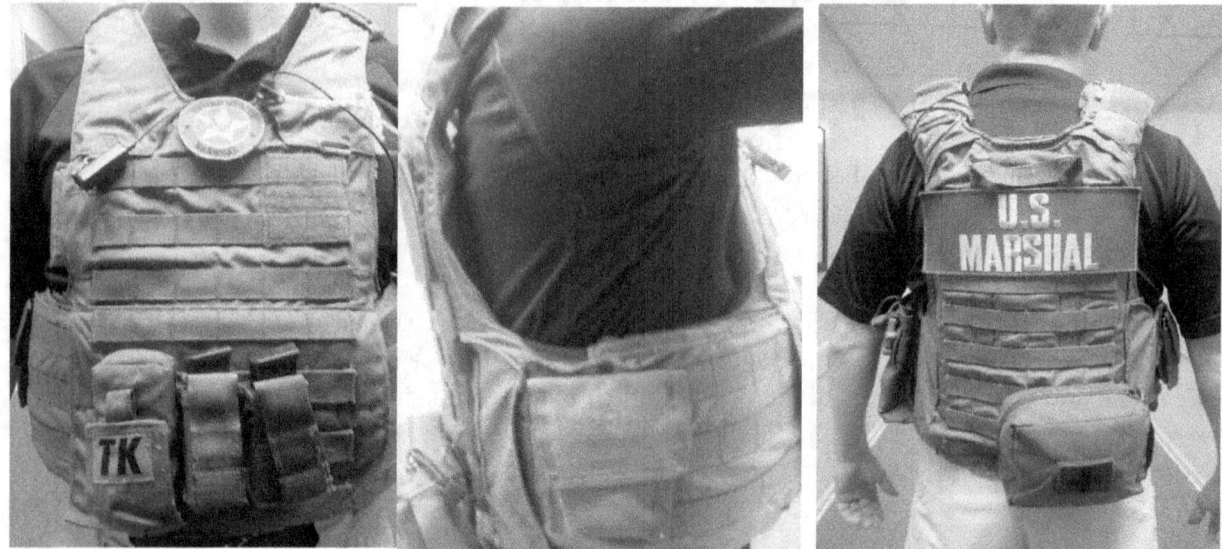

Pictured above is the Urban Assault Vest (UAV) typically used for task force operations and protective security details. The UAV includes a nylon vest (in green) and flexible armor panels inserted inside the nylon vest.

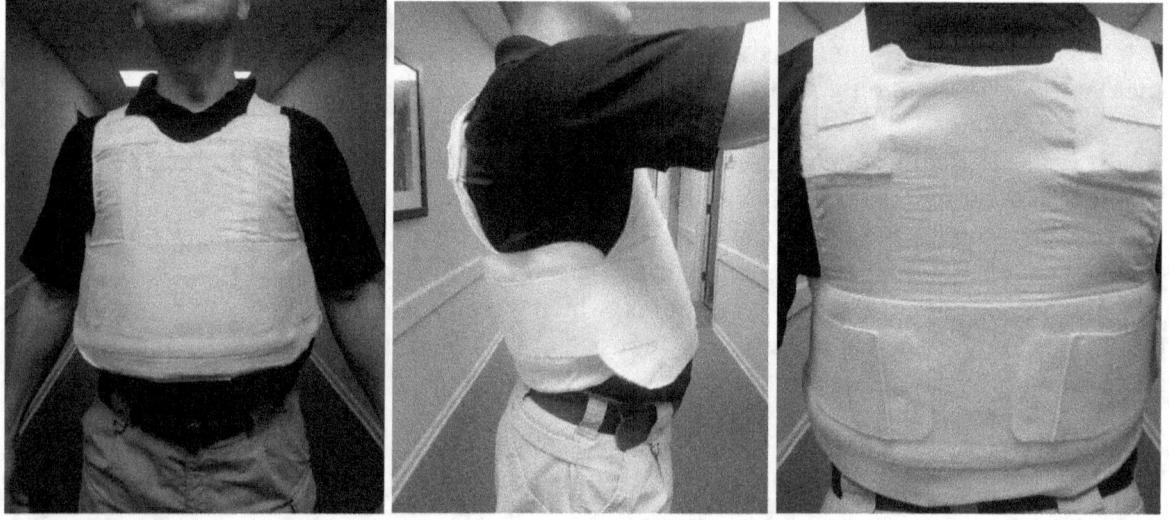

Pictured above is the Undercover Vest (UC) typically used in courtroom hearings or during surveillance operations. The UC includes a polyester (white) covering and flexible panels are inserted inside. The UC is worn underneath street clothes.

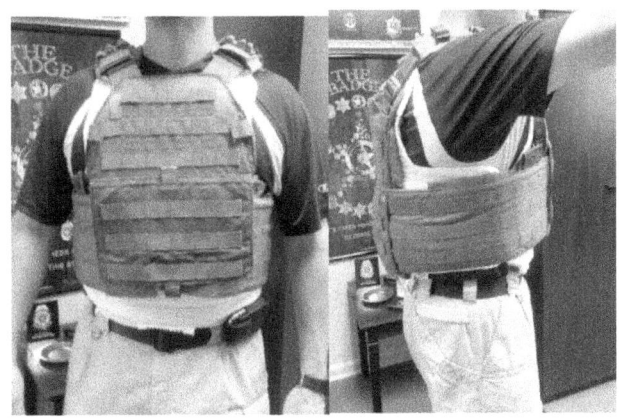

The Multi-Mission Armor Carrier (MMAC) plate carrier is pictured above. The MMAC is a nylon vest used for high-risk fugitive apprehensions and judicial security events. Rigid ballistic plates are inserted inside the front and back of the vest. The MMAC is worn on top of the Undercover Vest and provides maximum protection.

Item	Quantity	Unit Cost	Total Cost	Replacement Cycle	Annual Replacement Cost
Ballistic Plates and Panels	4,000	$1,100	$4,400,000	5 years	$880,000
Nylon Carriers	4,000	$500	$2,000,000	10 years	$200,000
New Deputies	100	$2,500	$250,000		$250,000
Total					**$1,330,000**

In 2013, the USMS conducted body armor testing to determine if the USMS should use the five-year warranty period as the agency's replacement cycle. The USMS determined that body armor panels less than five years old performed exceptionally well, with no penetration and low back-face deformation. Tests of armor that was over five years old resulted in 11 penetrations out of 84 shots taken, and unacceptable back-face deformation. Back-face deformation is an impact of the bullet on the back side of the armor; although the bullet does not penetrate the armor, the deformation would create significant blunt force trauma to the wearer.

In addition to examining body armor test results, the USMS also contacted other DOJ agencies regarding their replacement plans. DEA, FBI, and ATF confirmed that in general, their replacement cycles were consistent with the USMS replacement cycle. The USMS will continue to work with other DOJ components to test body armor based on National Institutes of Justice (NIJ) standards, and conduct additional tests beyond NIJ standards. For example, the USMS plans to add testing protocols to stop bullet fragments, water submersion, and climate variations.

Ballistic plates (both the flexible and rigid plates) are replaced every five years. The nylon carrier is replaced every 10 years. Establishing a normalized five-year replacement cycle for plates and a 10-year cycle for carriers requires **$1,330,000.**

ELECTRONIC SURVEILLANCE EQUIPMENT – $1,761,000

Technical surveillance equipment requires consistent funding to keep pace with the commercial wireless broadband industry. The USMS requests **$1,761,000** for the annual replacement of surveillance equipment to replace or upgrade its capabilities in the cellular surveillance arena as technology advances. The requested increase will maintain and improve electronic and technical surveillance techniques that enhance USMS investigative capabilities. USMS personnel have used this technology to capture the world's most wanted drug traffickers with no loss of life.

The TOG's missions involve lawful intercept of landline and cellular telephones, cellular geo location, GPS and radio frequency tagging/tracking, computer exploitation, computer forensics, and internet investigations including the lawful intercept of electronic mail and voice over internet protocol (VOIP). Without annual replacement funding for sound cyclical replacement, the TOG surveillance equipment inventory could reach block obsolescence once carriers convert to new technology. Should that occur, the USMS could forfeit its internationally-recognized technical investigative expertise and suffer a corresponding degradation to the success of its investigative responsibilities.

The lifecycle of surveillance equipment is directly related to technological advances in cellular protocols, particularly those used in the commercial wireless broadband industry. Technological changes also drive the requirement to update or replace surveillance equipment. For example, Sprint and T-Mobile have shut down older technology and migrated to new networks; since 2014, Verizon only sells smartphones that operate in the 4G Long Term Evolution (LTE) protocol; and AT&T has eliminated support for 2G Global System for Mobile (GSM) technology in 2017. Although LTE was intended to be the new standard for wireless protocols, carriers have already designed variations of that protocol (Verizon has already fielded its LTE Advanced network nationwide).

The Federal Government auction of 500 MHz spectrum to commercial broadband carriers and recent expansion of AWS III & IV spectrum has already extended frequencies and changed telecommunication networks beyond TOG's current electronic surveillance equipment capabilities. Telecommunications carriers are compelling the Third Generation Partnership Project (3GPP) working group to establish 5G network specifications would enable carriers to deploy 5G technologies by late 2019 and completely transition their networks to LTE and 5G by 2022. The 3GPP is a mobile communications industry collaboration that organizes and manages the standards and development of mobile communications standards. With no "finish line" in sight for technological advances, TOG's surveillance equipment requires a consistent funding source to keep pace with the ever changing commercial wireless broadband industry. USMS equipment must be upgraded to maintain current capabilities.

VEHICLE REPLACEMENT - $3,963,000

The USMS requests at least **$3,963,000** to fill critical shortages in the districts, and replace vehicles that have exceeded the USMS Vehicle Replacement Standards:

- Sedan Replacement Cycle – 7 years; 100,000 miles
- SUV/PU/Vans Replacement Cycle – 7 years; 100,000 miles
- Armored Vehicle Replacement Cycle – 5 years

The requested funding will allow the USMS to establish a consistent replacement schedule based on a reliable funding source. Four categories of vehicles are candidates for replacement:

- Vehicles which have met the age and mileage replacement standards. These vehicles have higher mileage resulting in higher maintenance costs.

- Vehicles that have not met age replacement standards but have excessive mileage. These vehicles incur higher maintenance costs as well.

- Aged vehicles that have not yet met current replacement standards due to lower mileage. These vehicles tend to have higher fuel consumption rates than current makes/models.

- Vehicle shortages throughout USMS districts. Specifically, there are critical needs in districts which do not have motor pool vehicles due to recent funding constraints. Motor pool vehicles serve as backups to replace those out of service due to unforeseen accidents or mechanical issues. 14 of 94 districts are not assigned a vehicle motor pool.

Category	Inventory Count	Unit Cost	Inventory Value	Replacement Standard	Annual Replacement Cost
Sedans	1,053	$20,272	$21,346,000	7 years 100,000 miles	$5,563,000
SUV / Pickup / Van	3,487	$25,903	$90,324,000	7 years 100,000 miles	$10,089,000
Armored Vehicle /1	185	$103,430	$19,135,000	5 years	$67,000
Vehicle Shortages	272	$28,500	$7,752,000	7 years 100,000 miles	$1,099,000
Total	**4,997**		**$138,556,704**		**$16,818,000**
/1 Armored vehicle replacement cost includes $40K for the vehicle and $63K for armor.					

The above table shows annual replacement cost for the entire USMS district fleet by category. Currently, the average USMS fleet vehicle is eight years old (FY 2009) with 51,105 miles. Average replacement cost is $26,000 per vehicle.

Impact on Performance

Cyclical Replacement Program

The request for base funding will allow the USMS to standardize its equipment replacement cycle to purchase much needed replacement of equipment that are likely past its normal useful cycle. Without requested base funding, the USMS will be unable to:

- Maintain a sound protective equipment and vehicle inventory, resulting in increased risk to operational personnel safety during performance of duties;

- Maintain access to critical information and data due to service disruptions; and

- Issue deputies vehicles and proper equipment to ensure reliable and secure communications during execution of critical missions.

Special Operations Group (SOG) Selection, Training, and Equipment

The USMS SOG cuts across all divisions and districts. As the primary tactical resource for the USMS, SOG supports DOJ and USMS operations throughout the nation and abroad. Ensuring SOG personnel are consistently well-trained and well-equipped is crucial to execution of the core missions and tasks assigned to the USMS by the Attorney General. The SOG's advanced training and superior equipment are the main reasons that USMS tactical teams are requested for special operations around the country.

Funding

Base Funding

FY 2016 Enacted				FY 2017 Continuing Resolution				FY 2018 Current Services			
Pos	Agt/ Atty	FTE	Amount ($000)	Pos	Agt/ Atty	FTE	Amount ($000)	Pos	Agt/ Atty	FTE	Amount ($000)
0	0	0	$0	0	0	0	$0	0	0	0	$0

Non-Personnel Increase/Reduction Cost Summary

Non-Personnel Item	Unit Cost ($000)	Quantity	FY 2018 Request ($000)	FY 2019 Net Annualization (change from 2018) ($000)	FY 2020 Net Annualization (change from 2019) ($000)
Body Armor	N/A	N/A	$1,330	$0	$0
Land Mobile Radios	N/A	N/A	$2,683	$0	$0
Vehicle Replacement	N/A	N/A	$3,963	$0	$0
SOG Selection, Mandatory Training & Recertification	N/A	N/A	$2,263	$0	$0
Electronic Surveillance Equipment	N/A	N/A	$1,761	$0	$0
Total Non-Personnel	N/A	N/A	$12,000	$0	$0

Total Request for this Item

Category	Pos	Agt/ Atty	FTE	Personnel ($000)	Non-Personnel ($000)	Total ($000)	FY 2019 Net Annualization (change from 2018) ($000)	FY 2020 Net Annualization (change from 2019) ($000)
Current Services	0	0	0	$0	$0	$0	N/A	N/A
Increases	0	0	0	$0	$12,000	$12,000	$0	$0
Total	0	0	0	$0	$12,000	$12,000	$0	$0

Item Name: **Immigration Enforcement Initiative**

Budget Decision Unit(s):   Judicial and Courthouse Security
                                  Fugitive Apprehension
                                  Prisoner Security and Transportation
                                  Protection of Witnesses
                                  Tactical Operations

Organizational Program: Immigration Enforcement

Program Increase: Positions 40 Agt/Atty 40 FTE 20 Dollars $8,755,000

Description of Item

The USMS requests **40 positions, 40 Deputy U.S. Marshals, 20 FTE, and $8,755,000** to support the President's January 25, 2017 Executive Order "Border Security and Immigration Enforcement Improvements." Implementation of the executive order is likely to increase the number of criminal aliens received into USMS custody. The requested positions will increase the number of Deputy U.S. Marshals dedicated to the increased immigration workload.

Justification

Funding increases for Department of Homeland Security (DHS) components and other additional law enforcement initiatives will dramatically expand the "front end" of the judicial pipeline. These pressures create immense pressure on DOJ as the DHS workload is compressed into the smaller DOJ end of the pipeline. Increased caseloads generated by Immigration and Customs Enforcement (ICE) and Customs and Border Protection (CBP) arrests need to be matched by concurrent resources for DOJ. Without additional funding, the USMS could turn into a "chokepoint" in the federal criminal justice process.

Not all CBP apprehensions are referred for criminal prosecution. Based on FY 2016 statistics, the referral rate is approximately 16.5% – of the 415,816 illegal entrants apprehended by the CBP, 68,731 were referred for criminal prosecution and subsequently housed by the USMS. If the volume of criminal referrals increases to 100,000 per year, the referral rate would be approximately 24%. Accordingly, if some portion of illegal entrance cases that have been previously been disposed of administratively are now prioritized for criminal prosecution, the number of prisoners in USMS custody could increase to more than historic levels.

An increase in immigration enforcement will increase the workload across USMS missions. Below are examples of the impact of the immigration executive orders on the USMS.

Prisoner Operations: Enforcement expansion will likely increase the number of USMS prisoners received and processed. The increased prisoner population will in turn generate additional prisoner housing and medical requirements and and a need for augmented prisoner ground and air transportation. The USMS responsibility for ensuring the integrity of the judicial process includes making in-custody defendants available for court proceedings and other judicial processes, and providing safe and secure prisoner housing. Reasonable proximity of prisoner housing to court facilities is essential to accomplishing this statutory requirement.

Judicial Security: An increase in the number of criminal aliens brought before the court will put a strain on court facilities and the judicial process. As these cases are ruled upon in federal court, the outcomes have potential to bring threats of, or actual, violence to judicial officers, witnesses, USMS employees, and facilities. Increased caseload and defendant counts are likely to result in threats to members of the judicial family, which will add to the number of predicated protective investigations and protective details. Increased courthouse traffic will impact security systems and personnel, including an increase to security and facility assessments and incidents.

Investigative Operations: Many USMS Regional Fugitive Task Forces and District Task Forces include DHS members (ICE, CBP, Homeland Security Investigations (HSI)). In the course of conducting fugitive investigations, USMS personnel may come into contact with individuals who are in violation of immigration laws. Those violations are either handled by DHS agents assigned to the task force or passed to appropriate DHS offices for action. The USMS District Task Forces conduct fugitive investigations when federal warrants have been issued for violations of criminal laws in certain immigration cases or violations of release conditions in immigration cases.

Impact on Performance

This initiative will enable the USMS to implement and maintain an integrated strategy that protects the federal judiciary, investigates warrants and arrests fugitives, and manages the prisoner workload resulting from increased immigration enforcement.

Funding

Base Funding

FY 2016 Enacted				FY 2017 Continuing Resolution				FY 2018 Current Services			
Pos	Agt/ Atty	FTE	Amount ($000)	Pos	Agt/ Atty	FTE	Amount ($000)	Pos	Agt/ Atty	FTE	Amount ($000)
1,332	1,032	1,294	$219,590	1,332	1,032	1,294	$224,578	1,185	918	1,152	$228,864

Personnel Cost Summary

Position/Series	Full Year Modular Cost per Position ($000)	1st Year Annualiz ation ($000)	Number of Positions Requested	FY 2018 Request ($000)	2nd Year ($000)	2nd Year FY 2019 Net Annualization (change from 2018) ($000)	3rd Year FY 2020 Net Annualization (change from 2019) ($000)
Criminal Investigative Series (1811)	$274	$219	40	$8,755	$7,891	-$864	$3,773
Total Personnel	$274	$219	40	$8,755	$7,891	-$864	$3,773

Total Request for this Item

Category	Pos	Agt/ Atty	FTE	Personnel ($000)	Non-Personnel ($000)	Total ($000)	FY 2019 Net Annualization (change from 2018) ($000)	FY 2020 Net Annualization (change from 2019) ($000)
Current Services	1,185	918	1,152	$204,101	$24,763	$228,864	N/A	N/A
Increases	40	40	20	$1,897	$6,858	$8,755	-$864	$3,773
Total	1,225	958	1,172	$205,998	$31,621	$237,619	-$864	$3,773

Item Name: **Violent and Gun-Related Crime Reduction Task Force**

Budget Decision Unit(s):   Fugitive Apprehension

Organizational Program: Fugitive Task Forces

Program Increase: Positions 0 Agt/Atty 0 FTE 0 Dollars $5,975,000

Description of Item

The USMS requests **$5,975,000** to support the President's February 9, 2017 Executive Order "Task Force on Crime Reduction and Public Safety." The task force was created by the Attorney General on February 28, 2017. The task force includes the Director of the Bureau of Alcohol, Tobacco, Firearms and Explosives (ATF), the Administrator of the Drug Enforcement Administration (DEA), the Director of the Federal Bureau of Investigation (FBI) and the Director of the U.S. Marshals Service (USMS). The task force is central to the Attorney General's commitment to combatting illegal immigration and violent crime, such as drug trafficking, gang violence, and gun crimes, and to restoring public safety to all of the nation's communities.

Justification

The Violent and Gun-Related Crime Reduction Task Force has a multi-agency focus on reducing violent and gun-related crime in particularly hard-hit urban areas by using innovative means to locate individuals, organizations and gangs within specific high crime jurisdictions. Federal law enforcement, including DEA, ATF and USMS will work with community leaders, educators, and local business owners to share information on identities, gang affiliation markers, and crime networking patterns with state and local law enforcement and members of the public. Resources will support the short-term deployment of federal law enforcement personnel to select urban areas to foster community awareness of criminal elements living, networking and thriving in their communities. Resources will also provide for convening town hall informational sessions, providing designated signage, communications, surveillance and monitoring equipment, and dedicated tip-lines and rewards in select high crime areas – and provide community and individual incentives for reporting crime to ensure violent and gun-related crime reduction is sustained long-term.

Impact on Performance

This initiative allows the USMS to more effectively reduce violent crime by prioritizing the apprehension of the most egregious violent fugitives. Additional resources will significantly improve the safety and effectiveness of arresting violent fugitives and enhance community safety.

Funding

Base Funding

FY 2016 Enacted				FY 2017 Continuing Resolution				FY 2018 Current Services			
Pos	Agt/ Atty	FTE	Amount ($000)	Pos	Agt/ Atty	FTE	Amount ($000)	Pos	Agt/ Atty	FTE	Amount ($000)
0	0	0	$0	0	0	0	$0	0	0	0	$0

Non-Personnel Increase

Non-Personnel Item	Unit Cost ($000)	Quantity	FY 2018 Request ($000)	FY 2019 Net Annualization (change from 2018) ($000)	FY 2020 Net Annualization (change from 2019) ($000)
Operational Expenses	N/A	N/A	$5,975	$0	$0
Total Non-Personnel	N/A	N/A	$5,975	$0	$0

Total Request for this Item

Category	Pos	Agt/ Atty	FTE	Personnel ($000)	Non-Personnel ($000)	Total ($000)	FY 2019 Net Annualization (change from 2018) ($000)	FY 2020 Net Annualization (change from 2019) ($000)
Current Services	0	0	0	$0	$0	$0	N/A	N/A
Increases	0	0	0	$0	$5,975	$5,975	$0	$0
Total	0	0	0	$0	$5,975	$5,975	$0	$0

VI. Program Offsets by Item

No program offsets.

www.ingramcontent.com/pod-product-compliance
Lightning Source LLC
Chambersburg PA
CBHW081237280526
45787CB00006B/2690